THE GLORY
OF THE
RESURRECTION

THE GLORY OF THE RESURRECTION

E. M. BOUNDS

BAKER BOOK HOUSE
Grand Rapids, Michigan

Copyright 1907 by Homer W. Hodge
Copyright 1921 by George H. Doran Company

Formerly published under the titles:
The Resurrection and *The Ineffable Glory*

Paperback edition issued 1978 by
Baker Book House Company

ISBN: 0-8010-0749-6

Printed in the United States of America

INTRODUCTION

The family Bible shows that the father of Rev. Edward M. Bounds, Thos. Jefferson Bounds, was born in Maryland Sept. 5th, 1801. His mother, Hester Ann Purnell, was born in Maryland. They married November 12th, 1823. Came to Kentucky, lived there for a few years, then moved to Marion County, Mo. Edward M. Bounds was born in Shelbyville, Mo., April the 15th, 1835. His father, Thos. J. Bounds, died and was buried in Shelby County. His mother died in 1882, June the 7th, and was buried in Kirksville, Mo.

Edward M. Bounds and his brother, Charles L., went to California under the lure of the gold discovery in 1849. Bounds was then only 14 years old. It is said that he and his brother were the only two boys who went across the plains—and carried their religion with them.

There were eight brothers and three sisters born to the family of Thos. J. Bounds, father of Edward M. Bounds. Edward M. studied law and was admitted and located in Hannibal, Mo., but the urgency to preach was so insistent that he gave up law after two years. He joined the Confederate Army at the opening of the war and was made a chaplain.

Bishop W. F. Mallalieu, having read these chapters on *The Resurrection*, said in 1908, "I have recently read two books by Rev. Edward M. Bounds. The classical quotations at the heads of the chapters are more than worth the money asked for the books. Bounds says the resurrection of Jesus Christ was complete, literal, entire and absolute; that the resurrection of the bodies of the dead, whatever disposition may be made of them, whether buried in the sea or burned to ashes, will be precisely analogous to the resurrection of the body of Jesus Christ."

I met this great saint in May, 1905, when he was 70 years old. He was then writing his *Preacher and Prayer* and these "thoughts on the Resurrection." We shared our board and bed with him off and on until he died. It was worth much to hear him talk. He would sit for hours in silent meditation and prayer and then begin in a delightful slow, sweet way, and if we broke in upon him he became very intense. To understand his meaning and his earnestness at times was painful. He coaxed us to rise with him at the 4 a. m. hour and wrestle for the lost world and for money to publish his books. At last God gave him the loan of enough money to publish

Preacher and Prayer and *The Resurrection* in 1907. The two books were written (figuratively speaking) in his blood and saturated through and through with his tears. Brother Bounds took his edition of *The Resurrection* home with him to Washington, Georgia, and there they remained locked up for 12 years. He wrote me in Brooklyn, N. Y., 15th Dec., 1911, these words, "These books I send you as a gift are my books on *The Resurrection*. They are God's great truths and will serve you well and any who read to refresh on that vital truth. On 21st Dec., 1911, he having so many of these books in his attic stored and no way to sell them, writes me these lines, "I send you via express twenty-five copies. They must be out preaching. They are God's truths. Choose your occasion and persons; give them away for God. I would like to see New York City sowed down with them." Scatter them as you can and more if you can and I will send them to you gladly. His longing soul knew the great hope of the Christian and he was interceding with God that his precious and priceless book might have readers for God's glory and God answered though ten years later, and now with a becoming binding and enterprising publishers one of the most glorious of all spiritual doctrines is opened and portrayed scripturally to a reading world who desire to read all he has ever written.

Dr. A. F. Scofield of London, England, in

studying the history of the Roman empire written by Polybius, the famed historian, discovered that the Roman army used three trumpet calls in breaking camp. First the trumpet blew loud and continuous for a few moments, which meant, "Strike your tents, pack your baggage, secure the animals." The second trumpet was to assemble the companies, battalions, in formation and await the last trumpet. The last trumpet was simply *"March."* The argument would run thus: Paul was among Roman soldiers at different places and even chained to one in Rome and had no doubt often heard the Three Trumpets sounding in the years gone among the victorious legions of imperial Rome. Being therefore familiar with the sound of the trumpets and their meaning he utters this marvelous statement in 1st Corinthians 15:52, in reference to the resurrection (thirty-five years before St. John wrote the 11th chapter of Revelations), "Behold I shew you a mystery; we shall not all sleep, but we shall all be changed, in a moment in the twinkling of an eye, at the *Last Trump."* The inference is that Paul made no reference at all to John's seventh trump in Revelations, but referred to the third trump of the Romans. If this hypothesis be true then we stand with those who are God's eagles. Having heard the first and second trump, we await the last command, "March," that we may be caught up together with them in the clouds to meet the Lord in the air: and so shall we ever be with the Lord."

Bounds' interpretation is that Christ will come to be glorified in all them that believe when that prayer of His shall be answered, "Father, I will that they whom Thou hast given me, be with me where I am, that they may behold my glory." He did not believe that Christ would come to be glorified in only a portion of His saints and admired only in so many of them that believe as have lived before the millennium, the rest to be brought in by degrees after Christ comes and to remain in the flesh as subjects of the former class.

Thank God that Christ purchased on the cross virtual redemption and actual redemption. Our Spirits have been virtually redeemed and actually redeemed: while the body has been only virtually redeemed. Ephesians 1:14: "Which is the earnest of our inheritance until the redemption of the *Purchased Possession.*" The purchased Possession is the body, it has not been actually redeemed until God glorifies it at the Resurrection. Then "the Lord Himself will descend from Heaven with a shout, with the voice of the archangel and with the trump of God: and the dead in Christ shall rise first. Then we which are alive and remain shall be caught up together with them in the clouds to meet the Lord in the air and so shall we ever be with the Lord. Wherefore comfort one another with these words." Glory be to God, Amen.

HOMER W. HODGE.

Brooklyn, N. Y.

CONTENTS

CHAPTER		PAGE
I.	Prefatory	15
II.	The Diurnal and Annual Resurrection	17
III.	The Whole Man Immortal	21
IV.	Christ the First Fruits of the Resurrection	28
V.	Death's Realms Invaded	35
VI.	Resurrection Power Lodged in Jesus Christ	40
VII.	God the Security: Resurrection Day Is a Pay Day	46
VIII.	"In Christ Shall All be Made Alive"	50
IX.	The Resurrection: The Essence of the Gospel	56
X.	The Judgment and the Resurrection	64
XI.	Not Another Body But the Same Body	70
XII.	A Literal Resurrection: The Bible Teaching	75

CHAPTER		PAGE
XIII.	Belief in the Resurrection as the Corner Stone of the Christian Dispensation	85
XIV.	Resurrection of the Body Complete	91
XV.	Wesley's Argument for a Resurrection and Not a Creation . . .	101
XVI.	The Christian's Body Raised Immortal and Incorruptible . .	109
XVII.	Some Bodies Will Shine More Brightly than Others . . .	116
XVIII.	Christ's Resurrection the Pledge and Symbol of Ours	121
XIX.	This Changed Body Will Never Know Weakness, Tears or Decay	126
XX.	And As We Have Borne the Image of the Earthy, We Shall Also Bear the Image of the Heavenly	131
XXI.	Our Bodies Changed Instantaneously at Second Coming of Christ	135
XXII.	Weariness, Waste, Weakness Here—Deathless Energy There . .	140

THE GLORY OF THE RESURRECTION

CHAPTER I

PREFATORY

I hear the thunder of eternity in my ears night and day: "Behold He cometh with clouds and every eye shall see Him, and they also which pierced Him; and all kindreds of the earth shall wail on account of Him; even so, amen."

Christ is near at hand for His prayer in the 17th chapter of St. John is evidently on the eve of being answered: "Father I will that they whom Thou hast given me be with me where I am, that they may behold my glory."
—Rev. Homer W. Hodge.

Besides the principles of which we consist and the actions which flow from us, the consideration of the things without us and the natural course of variations in the creature will render the resurrection yet more highly probable. Every space of twenty-four hours teacheth thus much in which there is always a revolution amounting to a resurrection. The day dies into night and is buried in silence and darkness; on the next morning it appeareth again and reviveth, opening the grave of darkness, rising from the dead of night. This is a diurnal resurrection. As the day dies into the night, so does the summer into winter; the sap is said to descend into the root, and there it lies buried in the ground; the earth is covered with snow or crusted with frost, and becomes a general sepulcher. When the spring appeareth, all begin to rise; the plants and flowers peep out of their graves, revive, and grow and flourish. This is the annual resurrection. The corn by which we live and for want of which we perish with famine is, notwithstanding, cast upon the earth and buried in the ground with a design that it may be corrupted and, being corrupted, may revive and multiply; our bodies are fed by this constant experiment, and we continue this life by a constant succession of resurrections. Thus all things are repaired by corrupting, are preserved by perishing, and revived by dying; and can we think that man, the lord of all these things which thus die and revive for him, should be detained in death, never to live again? Is it imaginable that God should thus restore all things to man, and not restore man to himself? If there were no other consideration but the principles of human nature, of the liberty and remunerability of human actions and of the natural revolutions and resurrections of other creatures, it were abundantly sufficient to render the resurrection of our bodies highly probable.—*Pearson on the Creed.*

CHAPTER II

THE DIURNAL AND ANNUAL RESURRECTION

Even the most illustrious [skeptic] has no better end than that of displaying his powers in confounding and darkening truth, and the happiest efforts of whose skepticism cannot be more leniently described than as brilliant feats of mental debauchery.
—SIR JAMES MACKINTOSH.

THE whole system of Jesus Christ is based on the immortality of the man. It is not the philosophical idea or guesses of the immortality of the soul, but the immortality of the man. The whole man, in his dual or triune nature, is to live forever. The spirit or higher department defies death; the body is to come out of the ruins and prison house of death and be raised to life. Man immortal; the whole man, soul, body, spirit, immortal—this is the keystone and keynote of the redemption by Christ. The deathless nature of the soul has been taught in the philosophies of earth, pagan and Christian, but the resurrection of the body is distinctively a Christian doctrine. It belongs to the revelation of God's Word. It is found in the Bible, and nowhere else. Nature may have echoes, analogies, figures;

but nowhere is the doctrine fully asserted, fully assured, but in the Scriptures which contain the revealed will of God.

This doctrine of the resurrection of the body is not a mere inference from Bible statement. It is the statement itself, the key of its arch, the corner stone of its foundation. It is not a rich afterthought of the gospel, but coördinate "Jesus and the resurrection" are the gospel.

Faith can make no appeal to reason or the fitness of things; its appeal is to the Word of God, and whatever is therein revealed faith accepts as true. Faith accepts the Bible as the word and will of God and rests upon its truth without question and without other evidence.

Faith accepts the Word of God as indubitable evidence of any fact, and rejoices in the fact as true because God asserts it in his Word. Many of the facts revealed to us in the Bible receive the credence of our reason as fit and proper things. Others extend beyond the range of reason, and it has neither vision nor analogy to measure them.

The resurrection of the human body, its coming back into life from the ravages, decay, and oblivion of the grave, is one of these supernatural facts. It has been the anxious and tearful question of the ages: "Can the dead live? Is there strength anywhere to vanquish death? Is there any hope of victory over the grave?" Reason has neither answer to the question nor hope for the questioner. Analogy starts some faint light, but this goes out amid the increasing night of the tomb.

There are but two questions to quicken and satisfy faith in the resurrection of the body. These questions are of promise and ability: Has God promised to raise the body from the dead? Is he able to perform his promise in this respect? The body is a distinct, a very important part of the man. It is the part seen, known, handled, described as the man, the organ, the outlet, through which the man comes into contact, sympathy, and action with the world around. A part, an all-important, indispensable part, of the man, the body belongs to the man, is an original, organic part of the man, evident and conspicuous —will this body rise from the dead where it has been laid amid tears and heart-breaking farewells? Its death is a fact distinct and clearly outlined. "Will it live again?" is the passionate question of love and longing.

The heathen world sighed out their upbraidings, emptiness, and despair. The flowers, said they, died by the chill of winter, but spring's warm breath brings them to life again. The day declines into darkness and night, but rises again into the full day; suns set, but come again fullorbed out of the eclipse of their setting; moons wane, but wax into fullness and brightness again;

but their loved ones leave them, eclipsed and lost in the darkness of death, but no spring, no morn, no rising ever brings them again.

Christianity hushes these sighs, fills this emptiness, lifts this despair. She lights the darkness of the grave with the morning star of hope, and sheds the luster of the resurrection day upon the night of the tomb. Faith asks of unbelief, of doubt and despair: "Why should it be thought a thing incredible with you that God should raise the dead? Is anything too hard for God?" She declares: "All that sleep in their graves shall hear the voice of the Son of God and shall come forth."

Faith puts the brightness of an immortal hope amid our graveyard griefs; writes on every tombstone, "I am the resurrection and the life;" calls aloud to every mourner, "Thy dead shall live." Christianity is not agnosticism, but faith, assurance, knowledge; not negative, but positive. "I believe in the resurrection of the body," is a fundamental and enduring item of her creed.

Christianity is not rationalism, but faith in God's revelation. A conspicuous, all-important item in that revelation is the resurrection of the body.

CHAPTER III

THE WHOLE MAN IMMORTAL

Present and future are alike bound up in our belief of our Lord's resurrection and ascension; and dreary indeed must this present be, and gloomy and clouded that future, if our belief in our risen and ascended Lord be uncertain, partial, precarious.—BISHOP ELLICOTT.

To the front, as the solid foundation for the resurrection of the body, is the resurrection of Jesus Christ. His resurrection opens the doors of the grave and lets in light and creates hope. "Go tell his disciples that he is risen." This angel announcement carries assurance and brightness to all earth's realms of doubt and death.

"The resurrection of Christ is the cause of our resurrection," as Pearson on the Creed says, "by a double causality as an efficient and an exemplary cause—as an efficient cause in regard that our Saviour by and upon his resurrection hath obtained power and right to raise all the dead, 'For as in Adam all die, even so in Christ shall all be made alive;' as an exemplary cause in regard that all the saints of God shall rise after the similitude and in conformity to the resurrection of Christ, 'For if we have been planted together in the likeness of his death, we shall be also in the likeness of his resurrection.' He shall change our vile bodies that they may be fashioned like unto his glorious body. As we have borne the image of the earthy, we may bear the image of the heavenly. This is the great hope of the Christian that Christ rising from the dead hath obtained the power and is become the pattern of his resurrection." Thy dead shall live; my dead bodies shall arise. Awake and sing, ye that dwell in the dust, for thy dew is as the dew of herbs, and the earth shall cast forth her dead.

The Scriptures link these two facts together, the resurrection of Jesus Christ from the dead and the resurrection of man's body from the grave. The dire results of his failing to rise, the gloom and wreck of an unrisen Christ is not too strongly put by an inspired writer: "Now if Christ be preached that he rose from the dead, how say some among you that there is no resurrection of the dead? But if there be no resurrection of the dead, then is Christ not risen: and if Christ be not risen, then is our preaching vain, and your faith is also vain. Yea, and we are found false witnesses of God; because we have testified of God that he raised up Christ: whom he raised not up, if so be that the dead rise not. For if the dead rise not, then is not Christ raised;

and if Christ be not raised, your faith is vain; ye are yet in your sins. Then they also which are fallen asleep in Christ are perished. If in this life only we have hope in Christ, we are of all men most miserable. But now is Christ risen from the dead, and become the first fruits of them that slept. For since by man came death, by man came also the resurrection of the dead. For as in Adam all die, even so in Christ shall all be made alive. But every man in his own order: Christ the first fruits; afterwards they that are Christ's at his coming."

Paul puts it strongly again: "For if we believe that Jesus died and rose again, even so them also that sleep in Jesus will God bring with him. But if the Spirit of him that raised up Jesus from the dead dwell in you, he that raised up Christ from the dead shall also quicken your mortal bodies by his spirit that dwelleth in you. And God hath both raised up the Lord, and will also raise up us by his own power. Knowing that he which raised up the Lord Jesus shall raise up us also by Jesus, and shall present us with you."

The Scriptures bear ample and continuous evidence that the faith of the resurrection of the body lies in the faith that Jesus Christ died and rose again. If his flesh rotted in the sepulcher of Joseph, then our hope of coming out of the grave rots also; if his body went to the dust of Palestine, then our faith, fancied faith and vaunted hope, of the resurrection is as pulseless and dead as dust.

All the simple and invincible proofs of the resurrection of Jesus Christ are confirmations deep, true, eternal as Holy Writ that our bodies, at the call of Jesus Christ, shall roll off the reproach and break the iron chains of death.

The resurrection of Jesus is the great affirming and cementing fact. By it he was declared to be the Son of God with power; it is the fitting and necessary complement to his advent and crucifixion; it binds into a complete whole all the facts of his wondrous life and puts the seal of truth on them; the keystone of the sacred arch, the crown of the system, the miracle of all miracles. It saves his crucifixion from scorn. It puts divinity and glory on the cross. The resurrection of Jesus Christ was necessary to establish the truth of his mission and put the stamp of all-conquering power on his gospel. His death met the law, conciliated divine justice; his resurrection sent the proclamation of liberty through all the realms of the dead and led the conqueror Death in chains.

The most casual reader of the New Testament can scarcely fail to see the commanding position the resurrection of Christ holds in Christianity. It is the creator of its new and brighter hopes, of its richer and stronger faith, of its deeper and more exalted experience. It is the salient point of New Testament preaching. "Jesus and the resurrection" summarized the subject of their sermonizing. Without this to them there was nothing but gloom and despair. If Christ, says the apostle, be not risen, then is our preaching vain, our faith vain, we are perjured as false witnesses for God, we are yet in our sins, our dead in Christ have perished hopelessly, and we are of all men most miserable. All these dire results are predicated of us if Christ be not risen. But the apostle arrests all these appalling consequences, and throws a flood of light and hope and life over the scene by this restatement and reassurance: "But now is Christ risen from the dead, and become the first fruits of them that slept." The resurrection of Christ reanimates our hopes of heaven and fixes them as sure as its foundations of adamant, and as precious and beautiful as its jeweled walls.

The resurrection of Jesus Christ is the birth of a new, glorious, immortal life on the realms of the midnight of death, the rising of the new sun on the terrors of darkness and night. It is the opening of a bright and noble highway to heaven where everything had been closed and sealed and every hope withered. Peter's rapturous acclaim is not the transport of impulse, but it is born of the most glorious and divine fact—a fact as solid and enduring as the granite of heaven, as enrapturing as the bliss and beauty of heaven.

The resurrection of Christ not only lifts darkness and dread from the tomb, but also spans the abyss which separates us from our loved dead, and puts into us the strength and hope of a glorious reunion in the very face of a separation the most painful, disastrous, and despairing.

The resurrection of Jesus both assures and patterns our resurrection; the two are conjoined. The nonresurrection of the body relegates Jesus back to his grave, and seals it as forever dead. Peter's triumphant shout plants the flower of immortality and life on every tombstone where faith had wrought its wondrous work.

"Blessed be the God and Father of our Lord Jesus Christ, who according to his great mercy begat us again unto a living hope by the resurrection of Jesus Christ from the dead, unto an inheritance incorruptible, and undefiled, and that fadeth not away, reserved in heaven for you, who by the power of God are guarded through faith unto a salvation ready to be revealed in the last time. Wherein ye greatly rejoice."

Hope throws its rich luster over the night of the tomb and thrills with deathless joy the heart where the resurrection of Jesus has been realized. We are to come out of the grave because Jesus came out of his grave. Our tombs will be empty of our bodies because Joseph's new tomb on the third morn was empty of his body. There is an inevitable, insuperable connection between the resurrection of Jesus Christ and the resurrection of our bodies.

The resurrection of Christ is the assurance and type of ours—his body which died, the same and not another, was raised. These bodies we now bear, the same ones we shall put in the grave, will be raised and fashioned after his glorious body. His resurrection takes the tyranny and sting from death, destroys its fears and vanquishes its dominion, brings the angels down beside our grave, plants hope and immortality on the ruins of that grave. His resurrection conquers for us a way through the dark domain of death; by it corruption puts on incorruption, mortality puts on immortality. Death is swallowed up, the victor's song is on our dying lips, and death becomes our coronation day.

CHAPTER IV

CHRIST THE FIRST FRUITS OF THE RESURRECTION

Never was there an age when it was more necessary to set forth events that not only imply but practically prove the resurrection of the body, and that not only suggest but confirm the teaching of the Church in reference to the future state which it is the obvious tendency of the speculations of our own times to explain away, to modify, or to deny.—BISHOP ELLICOTT.

IN the person of Jesus, his acts and teachings, death holds an essential, conspicuous place. It could not be otherwise. Death holds a commanding and ruinous reign over the race which Jesus Christ came to redeem. There could be no redemption of man without an invasion of the realms of death. No sunlight to humanity while the clouds and night of death hung heavy and dread, no spring bloom to man while the winter of death swept and froze with its polar blasts and killing frosts. The Emancipator must break the thrall which holds, throttles, and enslaves. Of his coming and of himself the long-away prophet had declared: "I will ransom them from the power of the grave: I will redeem them from death: O death, I will be thy plagues; O grave, I will be thy destruction." An age frivolous, recklessly treading on the verge of agnosticism and suicide, may reck nothing of death, its mystery and fear; but a serious age will open its eye and seriously and prayerfully confront death, recognize and lament its reign and ruin, as the king of terrors, the woe and blight of earth. Jesus Christ came to confront death, to war on death, to dismantle its empire, to discrown its king until every one of Christ's imprisoned ones shall shout: "Death is swallowed up in victory. O death, where is thy sting? O grave, where is thy victory?"

Jesus holds in his own person the death of death. He boldly declares: "If a man keep my saying, he shall never taste of death." He said in the presence of a death whose ruthless ravages had desolated his friendliest home and filled with bitterest grief his most devoted hearts: "I am the resurrection, and the life: he that believeth in me, though he were dead, yet shall he live: and whosoever liveth and believeth in me shall never die." He attested the wealth and glory of his triumph over death: "I am the first and the last, and the living one; and I was dead, and behold, I am alive for evermore, and I have the keys of death and of Hades."

What does Jesus, the great Teacher sent by God to teach us the great things of God, say about the rising again of the body from death? In raising the dead does he not in action and in plain, unmistakable fact declare his ability to raise the dead and intimate the possibility and encourage the hope of the resurrection? "And it came to pass the day after, that he went into a city called Nain; and many of his disciples went with him, and much people. Now when he came nigh to the gate of the city, behold, there was a dead man carried out, the only son of his mother, and she was a widow: and much people of the city was with her. And when the Lord saw her, he had compassion on her, and said unto her, Weep not. And he came and touched the bier: and they that bare him stood still. And he said, Young man, I say unto thee, Arise. And he that was dead sat up, and began to speak. And he delivered him to his mother. And there came a fear on all: and they glorified God, saying, That a great prophet is risen up among us; and, That God hath visited his people."

Is there not in this picture the doctrine of the resurrection of the dead? Is it not a prophecy and, even more, a pledge that death in all its forms shall be conquered? Shall he live and death reign? Does not this great miracle raise hope in him as the Lord of death? Can we not say, looking with wonderment on this display of the power of Jesus: "My flesh shall rest in hope?"

On his way to Jairus's house to heal his daughter, and while pausing to cure the woman with the issue of blood: "While he yet spake, there came from the ruler of the synagogue's house certain which said, Thy daughter is dead; why troublest thou the Master any further? As soon as Jesus heard the word that was spoken, he said unto the ruler of the synagogue, Be not afraid, only believe. And he suffered no man to follow him, save Peter, and James, and John the brother of James. And he cometh to the house of the ruler of the synagogue, and seeth the tumult, and them that wept and wailed greatly. And when he was come in, he saith unto them, Why make ye this ado, and weep? the damsel is not dead, but sleepeth. And they laughed him to scorn. But when he had put them all out, he taketh the father and the mother of the damsel, and them that were with him, and entereth in where the damsel was lying. And he took the damsel by the hand, and said unto her, Talitha cumi; which is, being interpreted, Damsel, (I say unto thee,) arise. And straightway the damsel arose, and walked; for she was of the age of twelve years. And they were astonished with a great astonishment. And he charged them straitly that no man should know it; and commanded that something should be given her to eat."

Another proof is this of his mastery over death that he has the keys of death and the fact that man's best friend has the power over man's greatest foe. It has that in it which gives hope over death, which does so readily yield to the power of Christ.

The other record of raising the dead is that of Lazarus. This is the crown of his miracles. Martha averred her belief in the fact of the general resurrection of the dead. "I know, said Martha, that he shall rise again in the resurrection at the last day. Jesus said unto her, I am the resurrection, and the life: he that believeth in me, though he were dead, yet shall he live: and whosoever liveth and believeth in me shall never die." Do not these words coupled with the action of Jesus give strong intimations and a well-grounded hope that Jesus will break the rule of death and bring light and immortality to light out of the midnight of the tomb? "And Jesus lifted up his eyes, and said, Father, I thank thee that thou hast heard me. And I knew that thou hearest me always; but because of the people which stand by I said it, that they may believe that thou hast sent me. And when he had thus spoken, he cried with a loud voice, Lazarus, come forth. And he that was dead came forth, bound hand and foot with graveclothes: and his face was bound about with a napkin. Jesus saith to them, Loose him, and let him go." How many others were raised from the dead is not recorded.

It seems an incident of common observation and the attestation of the divinity of his mission.

The raising from the dead of these persons is not only an attestation of the divinity of his mission, but we repeat that they are prophetical and proclamatory to the race of their emancipation from their fierce and relentless foe—death.

In addition to these acts which heralded the release of all incarcerated in the prison house of death, Jesus taught in express language the resurrection of the dead. His attitude toward death was one of dire and eternal opposition. He came as the representative of life and life-giving; that man might have life and have it more abundantly—a life unshadowed by death, and to which death was a stranger. In contrast and opposition to Adam, he was a life-giving Spirit. "Verily, verily, I say unto you, If a man keep my saying, he shall never see death." Again we refer to those wonderful words used in the presence of death, and in view of its iron rule, and while the tears of sympathy and indignation were still wet upon his cheeks he declared: "I am the resurrection and the life: he that believeth on me, though he were dead, yet shall he live: and whosoever liveth and believeth in me shall never die." These words find their highest and broadest truth: that in his very person there were forces and principles inimical and destructive to death; that, as he lived, death must die. The saying of Paul is but a condensed summary of this great purpose. "The appearing of our Saviour Jesus Christ, who hath abolished death, and hath brought life and immortality to light." The Epistle to the Hebrews asserts the same great truth: that in Jesus Christ, his person and his work, were lodged the mighty forces which were to bring universal freedom from death. "Forasmuch then as the children are partakers of flesh and blood, he also himself likewise took part of the same; that through death he might destroy him that had the power of death, that is, the devil; and deliver them who through fear of death were all their lifetime subject to bondage."

CHAPTER V

DEATH'S REALMS INVADED

I am not so ignorant of the temper and tendency of the age in which I live as either to be unprepared for the sort of remarks which the literal interpretation of the Evangelist will call, or to attempt an answer to them. Visionary ravings, obsolete whimsies, transcendental trash, and the like I leave to pass.—S. T. COLERIDGE.

THE attitude of Jesus Christ to the doctrine of the resurrection of the dead is one of familiarity and matter of course. In the sixth chapter of John with what an emphatic, authoritative manner he deals with it as a generally acknowledged, great basic fact! "For I came down from heaven, not to do mine own will, but the will of him that sent me. And this is the Father's will which hath sent me, that of all which he hath given me I should lose nothing, but should raise it up again at the last day."

This resurrection he puts as the declared purpose and will of God, that he should raise them up at the last day. This was imperative if he accomplishes God's design. The capsheaf of God's purposes for Jesus Christ was that he should raise the dead. Again he returns to this great thought, purpose, and fact: "And this is the will of him that sent me, that every one which seeth the Son, and believeth on him, may have everlasting life: and I will raise him up at the last day."

Again he iterates the fact, and declares that he is committed to it. The Father commits it to him. The resurrection power is lodged in Jesus. "No man can come to me, except the Father which hath sent me draw him: and I will raise him up at the last day." Again Jesus gives utterance to the important statement: "Whoso eateth my flesh, and drinketh my blood, hath eternal life; and I will raise him up at the last day."

Death and him that had the power of death —that is, the devil—against these, the author of evil and his works, Jesus Christ set himself. He declared himself to be the resurrection and the life, that death in every form, in every way, and at every place, must yield to him. We stress and iterate the fact that he is life. "If a man keep my saying, he shall never see death." "Whosoever liveth and believeth in me shall never die." "He that believeth in me, though he were dead, yet shall he live." "I am the first and the last, and the Living one; and I was dead, and behold, I am alive for evermore, and I have the keys of death and of Hades." "I am come that they might have life, and have it more abundantly." Life against death is he. Jesus Christ, the source of all deathless energy, by absolute and eternal fitness, by a matter of course, and by character he is the foe, the destruction of death. He is coequal, coeternal with the Father, and pours the Father's full tide of life on the world. "For the Father loveth the Son, and showeth him all things that himself doeth: and he will show him greater works than these, that ye may marvel. For as the Father raiseth up the dead, and quickeneth them; even so the Son quickeneth whom he will. For the Father judgeth no man, but hath committed all judgment unto the Son: Verily, verily, I say unto you, He that heareth my word, and believeth on him that sent me, hath everlasting life, and shall not come into condemnation; but is passed from death unto life. Verily, verily, I say unto you, The hour is coming, and now is, when the dead shall hear the voice of the Son of God: and they that hear shall live. For as the Father hath life in himself; so hath he given to the Son to have life in himself; And hath given him authority to execute judgment also, because he is the Son of man."

"Marvel not at this: for the hour is coming, in the which all that are in the tombs shall hear his voice, and shall come forth: they that have done good, unto the resurrection of life; and they that have done ill, unto the resurrection of judgment." He had made strong declarations of life, eternal life, and of a spiritual resurrection; seeing their wonderment, he goes on to declare a greater marvel still—the resurrection of the body from the grave as the inevitable sequence of the life in his Father and in himself. All shall come forth —death shall yield its hold, and the grave deliver its prisoners long held. All shall come forth— not a body left—not an atom of the grave's dust but shall have the touch and taste of the resurrection life. Jesus Christ tells his disciples that when he comes in the glory of his Father with the holy angels he will reward every man according to his works. To secure this end, the resurrection is a necessity.

The transfiguration of Jesus is one of the typical facts of the resurrection of the body; not only of the glorious change, but of the renewed life of the body and of the general judgment day. The presence of Moses and Elijah there are the trophies as they appear in glory of the resurrection power of Christ. It is a distinct prophecy and foreshadowing of the coming of the body out of the power and ravages of death. Moses and Elijah appear at this hour as the first fruits of the resurrection glory. It is worthy of remark that it is here as well as in the continuous ministry of Christ that the body, this body of our humiliation, has its sign and pledge of its future glory.

"I will raise him up at the last day." These

iterated words deserve great and grave consideration—there is to be a day, a great day, a tremendous day; the last day, the closing of this world's history. Time shall be no more. Eternity, changeless eternity, will begin its new history for man. Paul calls it "the day of wrath and revelation of the righteous judgment of God;" the day when "the dead, small and great, shall stand before God." The raised dead—raised from their sleep in proud city cemetery or the silent forsakenness of the unmarked loneliness of the country sleeper; from the ocean depths, shrouded and entombed for ages in its restless, defiant, fathomless caves; from the dismal abodes of the Hades whose waves and fires were but the voices which told of deeper waves and fiercer fires to come. This is the day when Christ is committed to the raising of his dead ones, when his and man's last enemy, death, shall be destroyed.

"Last day!" Day of God's glory and power! Day of terror and alarm to the unbelieving and impenitent—their eternal doom! Day of renown and victory to Jesus Christ, of infinite comfort to all his saints. Infinite comfort! Infinite in measure and infinite in length. This last day is one of God's appointed days—God's decreed days.

CHAPTER VI

RESURRECTION POWER LODGED IN JESUS CHRIST

The power of God speaks it possible that there may be a resurrection; the Scriptures make it certain that there shall be a resurrection.—REV. MATTHEW HENRY.

If you knew the power of God, you would know that He can do it; and if you knew the Scriptures, you would know that He will do it.—BISHOP HORNE.

IN the lessons that Jesus Christ taught of the unselfish ministries of the social life he guards our feasts and their guests so that there may be none of the pride of life in them: "Then said he also to him that bade him, When thou makest a dinner or a supper, call not thy friends, nor thy brethren, neither thy kinsmen, nor thy rich neighbors; lest they also bid thee again, and a recompense be made thee. But when thou makest a feast, call the poor, the maimed, the lame, the blind: and thou shalt be blessed; for they cannot recompense thee: for thou shalt be recompensed at the resurrection of the just."

The resurrection of the dead was an accepted fact in Jewish popular teaching and credence, well known and constantly taught in the Pharisaic schools of thought and doctrine, grounded on the teaching of the Old Testament and their schools of tradition and stalwart orthodoxy. In teaching, Christ accepts as true the doctrine as understood and so bases and refers the holy ministries of mercy and service to that great time for their recompense: "At the resurrection of the just."

All the events of this life are to have their reference to the resurrection hour! How unselfish and dignified, how full of gravity will a life be that shapes all its actions by the resurrection or judgment day! "But I say unto you, That every idle word that men shall speak, they shall give account thereof in the day of judgment. For by thy words thou shalt be justified, and by thy words thou shalt be condemned." *"Thou shalt be recompensed at the resurrection of the just."* Assured fact! The truth of all truths! Let us keep our eye on that great hour. Let us shape our actions by its high rules of righteousness, rectitude, truth! Let us await its awards with a holy, lowly, unselfish ministry to the afflicted and beggared ones of earth, who cannot recompense us—take God as their security, and look to the resurrection as pay day.

The statements of Jesus are direct in regard to the resurrection of the dead. The Sadducees, who did not believe in the resurrection, propounded a question to Christ in order to confute the doctrine. In his reply he asserts the fact in opposition to the Sadducees and elevates the doctrine above the low and carnal views of the Pharisees, and also asserts it as fundamental to the nature of God and as belonging to the teachings of Moses.

"Then came to him certain of the Sadducees, which deny that there is any resurrection; and they asked him, saying, Master, Moses wrote unto us, If any man's brother die, having a wife, and he die without children, that his brother should take his wife, and raise up seed unto his brother. There were therefore seven brethren: and the first took a wife, and died without children. And the second took her to wife, and he died childless. And the third took her: and in like manner the seven also: and they left no children, and died. Last of all the woman died also. Therefore in the resurrection whose wife of them is she? for seven had her to wife. And Jesus answering said unto them, The children of this world marry, and are given in marriage: but they which shall be accounted worthy to obtain that world, and the resurrection from the dead, neither marry, nor are given in marriage: neither can they die any more: for they are equal unto the angels; and are the children of God, being the children of the resurrection. Now that the dead are raised, even Moses showed at the bush, when he calleth the Lord the God of Abraham, and the God of Isaac, and the God of Jacob. For he is not a God of the dead, but of the living: for all live unto him."

This afforded Jesus Christ a fine opportunity to explode the doctrine of the resurrection if not true; instead he relieves the doctrine of its Pharisaic rubbish and debauchment, declares and confirms it by Scripture and by the character of God, putting it upon its divine and spiritual basis.

This is an important occasion. It is light on the doctrine of the resurrection to those who opposed it. Doubtless this question had often confused and silenced the Pharisees. The Sadducees denied the resurrection—angel and spirit. Here they came saying there was no resurrection, maintaining this against our Lord. He answers: "Ye do not understand the Scriptures which imply the resurrection, nor the power of God before which all these obstacles vanish." Our Lord asserts here against the Sadducees the existence of angels and reveals to us the similarity of our future glorified state to their present one. The books of Moses were the great and ultimate appeal for all doctrine. The assertion of the resurrection comes from the very books from which their objections had been constructed. Our Lord here speaks of the conscious intent of God in speaking the words. God uttered these words to Moses in the consciousness of the still enduring existence of his peculiar relation to Abraham, Isaac, and Jacob. Jesus declares that they still live. It is an assertion which could not be made of an annihilated being of the past. Weighty testimony against the so-called sleep of the soul in the intermediate state. The burden of the law, "I am the Lord thy God," contains in it the seed of immortality and the hope of the resurrection.

For the present state of men marriage is an ordained and natural state of things. They who are worthy to obtain the resurrection life are no longer under the ordinance of marriage, for neither can they die any more. They will have no need of a succession and renewal; they are alive for evermore. They are by their resurrection essentially partakers of the divine nature, and can die no more. It is a covenant relation on which the matter rests. In regard to him who inhabiteth eternity, the being of all is a living one in all its changes. (Alford's "Commentary on Matthew and Luke.")

How clearly, distinctly, sublimely our Lord declares the resurrection of the body from God's relation to his covenant patriarchs, as shown in the call of Moses for their deliverance from an enslavement as dark, as terrible, and as hopeless as death! Their deliverance from the death and slavery of Egypt was to be a type and prophecy of the glory of the resurrection from the dominion and tyranny of death.

Our Lord on this occasion, answering the questioning of the Sadducees, puts them to silence;

but beyond this he draws the sublimest lesson about the great doctrine of the resurrection of the body, from the call of Moses, and unfolds the truth free from the stain and thralls of the flesh. The resurrection—heavenly life—is to be a new life based on new relations. The earthly family institutions are not to be revived in the resurrection life. They have their divine uses on earth, pass their day here, but will not have their place in the eternal. The angel life will be the model. The angels are not born into families; each one is separate, independent. So will be our future, individualized and immortal. No marriage there —marriage, the basis of earthly relations, the prime factor in earthly good, will not be there. No death—the source of deepest woe and pain will not be there. Marriage and death are earthly and not heavenly—belong to earth and not to heaven.

CHAPTER VII

GOD THE SECURITY: RESURRECTION DAY IS A PAY DAY

Had Jesus Christ delivered no other declaration than the following, "Marvel not at this: for the hour is coming, in the which all that are in the graves shall hear his voice, and shall come forth; they that have done good, unto the resurrection of life; and they that have done evil, unto the resurrection of damnation," He had pronounced a message of inestimable importance and well worthy of that splendid apparatus of prophecy and miracle with which His mission was introduced and attested—a message in which the wisest of mankind would rejoice to find an answer to their doubts and rest to their inquiries.

—S. T. COLERIDGE.

THE bringing back of the dead is one of the great distinctive and gloriously magnificent and triumphant facts of the gospel—its glory, the crown and seal of its divinity. If the dead rise not, its scepter is departed, its prophecies and promises have failed, its luster is dimmed and tarnished, its melody turned to discord and shame. The resurrection is to the world what the minstrel was to Elisha. All prophecies, all visions of beauty, the hand of the Lord—all are in it. If the dead rise not, then are we most miserable, tuneless, and dead—neither inspiration, vision, prophecy, nor God with us. This great fact is iterated and reiterated by new statement, by figure, and by type. It is the theme which checks the sigh, comforts the mourner, makes strong the weak, lights the fires of immortality and eternal life amid the darkness and ravages of earth's graveyards, spans the dark abyss of death with the golden bridge of an eternal reunion, spirit and body both in heaven.

A simple setting will show how large a place the resurrection of the body had in the preaching, experience, hopes, and comforts of the New Testament Christians.

Jesus Christ had in his person the power of the resurrection. He was the incarnation of the resurrection. Yet outside of his person there was the fact of the resurrection. The power in him, his resurrection applied, brings into life again all the dead. "As in Adam all die, even so in Christ shall all be made alive." How clear and strong is the statement about the Holy Spirit in us, whose indwelling gives to us the pledge and verity of the resurrection as well as the earnest of heaven! "But if the Spirit of him that raised up Jesus from the dead dwell in you, he that raised up Christ from the dead shall also quicken your mortal bodies by his Spirit that dwelleth in you."

So we come into sympathy with struggling, groaning, oppressed creation about us, which has in its very groans the prophecy of its resurrection. Nature in this says that the divine word is but a figure of us looking with oppressed and eager groanings to the future. "For the earnest expectation of the creature waiteth for the manifestation of the sons of God. For the creature was made subject to vanity, not willingly, but by reason of him who hath subjected the same in hope. Because the creature itself also shall be delivered from the bondage of corruption into the glorious liberty of the children of God. For we know that the whole creation groaneth and travaileth in pain together until now. And not only they, but ourselves also, which have the first fruits of the Spirit, even we ourselves groan within ourselves, waiting for the adoption, to wit, the redemption of our body. For we are saved by hope: but hope that is seen is not hope: for what a man seeth, why doth he yet hope for? But if we hope for that we see not, then do we with patience wait for it."

This is the prophecy, poetry, and bloom of Christ's system. The future is its glory. The resurrection is the rich jewel of the gospel. The Holy Spirit inspires nature and fills man with this glorious resurrection hope. The more we have of the power of the Spirit's inworking, the deeper and stronger are the convictions of the resurrection; and the richer, sweeter, more assured the consciousness of our salvation by hope, the more profound the certainty of the adoption of these bodies into the glorious familyhood of the heavenly home.

The Sadducees denied the resurrection of the dead. That which inflamed and grieved them and aroused them to unite with the enemies of the disciples was that the disciples taught and preached through Jesus the resurrection from the dead. Apostolic teaching and preaching broadened the resurrection from the personal resurrection of Jesus to the universal fact of the resurrection of the dead. As certainly as Jesus had been raised from the dead, so certainly would all the dead be raised.

CHAPTER VIII

"IN CHRIST SHALL ALL BE MADE ALIVE"

Skepticism must ever be a misfortune or defect: a misfortune if there be no means of arriving at truth; a defect if, while there exists such means, we are unable or unwilling to use them.—THOMAS ARNOLD.

THE doctrine of the resurrection of the dead was emphasized by Paul and made most conspicuous as being the essence and sum of the gospel. In Athens—cultured, skeptical, proud Athens—he declares the great fact. It brought a new life and a new and unknown hope to the paganized world: "Now while Paul waited for them at Athens, his spirit was stirred in him, when he saw the city wholly given to idolatry. Therefore disputed he in the synagogue with the Jews, and with the devout persons, and in the market daily with them that met with him. Then certain philosophers of the Epicureans, and of the Stoics, encountered him. And some said, What will this babbler say? others said, He seemeth to be a setter forth of strange gods: because he preached unto them Jesus, and the resurrection."

Mars Hill heard the same before its august

tribunal: "And the times of this ignorance God winked at; but now commandeth all men everywhere to repent: because he hath appointed a day, in the which he will judge the world in righteousness by that man whom he hath ordained; whereof he hath given assurance unto all men, in that he hath raised him from the dead. And when they heard of the resurrection of the dead, some mocked: and other said, We will hear thee again of this matter."

Before the Jewish council he declared: "Of the hope and resurrection of the dead I am called in question."

Paul's address before the Roman governor, Felix, was a personal defense, yet made strong by the doctrine of the resurrection which he declared to be his main offense. "But this I confess unto thee," he declares, "that after the way which they call heresy, so worship I the God of my fathers, believing all things which are written in the law and in the prophets: and have hope toward God, which they themselves also allow, that there shall be a resurrection of the dead, both of the just and unjust."

In the same address he returns to and dwells on this fact of raising the dead: "Let these same here say, if they have found any evil doing in me, while I stood before the council, except it be for this one voice, that I cried standing among them, Touching the resurrection of the dead I am called in question by you this day."

He asserted before Agrippa that the doctrine of the resurrection was the great promise of God to the fathers, the promise which gave hope to them and hope and fortitude to him; and then startles the Romanized Jewish judge by the question: "Why should it be thought a thing incredible with you, that God should raise the dead?"

The doctrine of the resurrection of the dead was everywhere preached and believed as one of the primary, fundamental, all-inclusive facts of the gospel. It comes in also incidentally as well as doctrinally. It comes to give largeness and power to experience; to give point and force to an exhortation or injunction. "Now the body is not for fornication, but for the Lord; and the Lord for the body. And God hath both raised up the Lord, and will also raise up us by his own power. Know ye not that your bodies are the members of Christ?" But we had the sentence of death in ourselves, that we should not trust in ourselves, but in God which raiseth the dead." Again: "We having the same spirit of faith, according as it is written, I believed, and therefore have I spoken; we also believe, and therefore speak; knowing that he which raised up the Lord Jesus shall raise up us also by Jesus, and shall present us with you."

Some members of the Corinthian Church had

fallen into error about the resurrection of the dead. The fifteenth chapter of First Corinthians is devoted to the refutation of their errors and the statement of the doctrine. Therein the apostle views it from almost every standpoint and with all colors. The fact of death so universal and deplorable is centered in Adam; the fact of the resurrection, its truth, authority, and glory, centers in Christ: "For since by man came death, by man came also the resurrection of the dead. For as in Adam all die, even so in Christ shall all be made alive. But every man in his own order: Christ the first fruits; afterwards they that are Christ's at his coming. Then cometh the end, when he shall have delivered up the kingdom to God, even the Father; when he shall have put down all rule and all authority and power. For he must reign, until he hath put all enemies under his feet. The last enemy that shall be destroyed is death. For he hath put all things under his feet. But when he saith, all things are put under him, it is manifest that he is excepted, which did put all things under him. And when all things shall be subdued unto him, then shall the Son also himself be subject unto him that put all things under him, that God may be all in all."

He declares: "In a moment, in the twinkling of an eye, at the last trump: for the trumpet shall sound, and the dead shall be raised incorruptible, and we shall be changed. For this corruptible must put on incorruption, and this mortal must put on immortality."

The following majestic, luminous, and comforting declarations were made to the Thessalonians: "But I would not have you to be ignorant, brethren, concerning them which are asleep, that ye sorrow not, even as others which have no hope. For if we believe that Jesus died and rose again, even so them also which sleep in Jesus will God bring with him. For this we say unto you by the word of the Lord, that we which are alive and remain unto the coming of the Lord shall in no wise precede them which are asleep. For the Lord himself shall descend from heaven with a shout, with the voice of the archangel, and with the trump of God: and the dead in Christ shall rise first: then we which are alive and remain shall be caught up together with them in the clouds, to meet the Lord in the air: and so shall we ever be with the Lord. Wherefore comfort one another with these words."

What a place the resurrection of the dead had in apostolic preaching! What comfort and solaces it had! How oft repeated to edify, refresh, strengthen! What a rich message it was for the early Church to bear and receive! What a volume full of inspiration and embellished to them! How oft repeated! how well assured were they of its truth! It belonged to the heart of their faith; it burnished with a double radiance their hopes;

it made them to endure martyr fires and persecutions fiercer than martyr flames! We need to have these first fundamental facts put into our spiritual being anew like iron put into the blood to make it red and strong and life-giving. These mighty fact-forces have to us lost their energy and their divine magic. Our faith demands to be fed anew by them. They must be to us what they were to the apostles—the summary, subject, and power of our preaching. They must be to us the pabulum of our faith, the food of our souls, the nurser of a giant faith, the inspirer of giant praying.

These facts must be to us what they were to the primitive Christians—creed, experience, service. They must weave our songs, fill our testimony. We must know that Jesus Christ has been raised from the dead, for we have been raised from the death of sin with him. We must know that our bodies shall be raised from the dead by his Spirit which is in us, which gives an assurance and foretaste of the resurrection day.

> O what a blessed hope is ours!
>   While here on earth we stay,
> We more than taste the heavenly powers,
>   And antedate that day:
> We feel the resurrection near,
>   Our life in Christ concealed,
> And with his glorious presence here
>   Our earthen vessels filled.

CHAPTER IX

THE RESURRECTION: THE ESSENCE OF THE GOSPEL

I am laboring, though most imperfectly, to lead them (my scholars) to Christ in true and devoted faith. I hold all the scholarship that ever man had to be infinitely worthless in comparison with even a very humble degree of spiritual advancement.—THOMAS ARNOLD OF RUGBY.

THE resurrection of the body will be universal and personal, general and particular, of every one good and bad, or, in the language of the Bible, "a resurrection of the just and unjust." It will take place generally and at the last day. Jesus Christ is very clear in his statement as to the time.

He declares his supreme loyalty to the Father, and avers, "I came down from heaven not to do mine own will, but the will of him that sent me," and then declares the will of his Father in regard to the resurrection: "And this is the Father's will which hath sent me, that of all which he hath given me I should lose nothing, but should raise it up again at the last day."

With great solemnity he again declares the will of the Father and his own power and purpose in raising all believers from the dead "at the last day:" "And this is the will of him that sent me, and every one which seeth the Son, and believeth on him, may have everlasting life: and I will raise him up at the last day."

He combines it with the statement of the Father's drawing, and the drawn ones are to be raised "at the last day:" "No man can come to me, except the Father which hath sent me draw him: and I will raise him up at the last day." And again he iterates and reasserts that the crowning glory is to be the resurrection at the last day: "Whoso eateth my flesh, and drinketh my blood, hath eternal life; and I will raise him up at the last day."

This was the accepted truth of the resurrection stated by Martha in her great sorrow at Lazarus's death: "I know that he shall rise again in the resurrection at the last day." Again Jesus uses the statement which locates the resurrection and combines it with the judgment: "He that rejecteth me, and receiveth not my words, hath one that judgeth him: the word that I have spoken, the same shall judge him in the last day."

These two tremendous facts—the judgment and the resurrection—are united in God's Word. They certainly have a close unity in importance, in event, and in bearing. Peter declared of Christ: "He which is charged of God to be judge of the quick and dead." Paul in his solemn charge to Timothy declares of Jesus that he shall judge the quick and the dead at his appearing and kingdom. Peter, in his Epistle, says: "Who shall give account to him that is ready to judge the quick and the dead."

There can be no doubt that in the plain teaching of Jesus and his apostles these two facts, resurrection and judgment, are united. "Wherefore we labor, that, whether present or absent, we may be accepted of him. For we must all appear before the judgment seat of Christ; that every one may receive the things done in his body, according to that he hath done, whether it be good or bad. Knowing therefore the terror of the Lord, we persuade men." The saints are specially charged and reminded that they must appear before the judgment seat of Christ for the things done in the *body*. In the interest of compassion and love, in our judgment, Paul in Romans interrogates and reminds Christians: "But why dost thou judge thy brother? or why dost thou set at naught thy brother? for we shall all stand before the judgment seat of Christ. But he that judgeth me is the Lord. Wherefore judge nothing before the time, until the Lord come, who will both bring to light the hidden things of darkness, and make manifest the counsels of the heart; and then shall each man have his praise from God."

To heal broken hearts, to confirm faith, to

arrest excessive mourning for our dead, Paul gives utterance to the Thessalonians: "But I would not have you to be ignorant, brethren, concerning them which are asleep, that ye sorrow not, even as others which have no hope. For if we believe that Jesus died and rose again, even so them also which sleep in Jesus will God bring with him. For this we say unto you by the word of the Lord, that we which are alive and remain unto the coming of the Lord shall not prevent them which are asleep. For the Lord himself shall descend from heaven with a shout, with the voice of the archangel, and with the trump of God: and the dead in Christ shall rise first: then we which are alive and remain shall be caught up together with them in the clouds, to meet the Lord in the air: and so shall we ever be with the Lord. Wherefore comfort one another with these words."

In the fact of a general judgment as well as in the coming of our Lord, the resurrection of the dead is held as a fact precedent and to be taken for granted. This is declared in the parable of the talents, the lord coming to reckon with his servants. This purpose had been declared and established from the first: "And Enoch also, the seventh from Adam, prophesied of these, saying, Behold, the Lord cometh with ten thousand of his saints."

We have Christ's inimitable description of his

coming the object in the twenty-fifth chapter of Matthew: "When the Son of man shall come in his glory, and all the holy angels with him, then shall he sit upon the throne of his glory: and before him shall be gathered all nations: and he shall separate them one from another, as a shepherd divideth his sheep from the goats: and he shall set the sheep on his right hand, but the goats on the left."

His dual purpose is set forth to the disquieted Thessalonians in strong terms, and they are urged to repose under the cheering fact that their Saviour would come again, and his coming would be to them the end of sorrow, of pain, and fear: "And to you who are troubled rest with us, when the Lord Jesus shall be revealed from heaven with his mighty angels. In flaming fire taking vengeance on them that know not God, and that obey not the gospel of our Lord Jesus Christ: who shall be punished with everlasting destruction from the presence of the Lord, and from the glory of his power; when he shall come to be glorified in his saints, and to be admired in all them that believe."

"And I saw the dead, small and great, stand before God; and the books were opened: and another book was opened, which is the book of life: and the dead were judged out of those things which were written in the books, according to their works. And the sea gave up the dead which were in it; and death and hell delivered up the dead which were in them: and they were judged every man according to their works. And death and hell were cast into the lake of fire. This is the second death. And whosoever was not found written in the book of life was cast into the lake of fire."

"And the times of this ignorance God winked at; but now commandeth all men everywhere to repent: because he hath appointed a day, in the which he will judge the world in righteousness by that man whom he hath ordained; whereof he hath given assurance unto all men, in that he hath raised him from the dead."

All these passages of the judgment are promises and pledges of the resurrection of the dead. The Bible is explicit on the point; no vague analogies, no poetic dreams, but plain statement declaring the fact.

The resurrection will be general, all will be raised at the same time, as Paul declares—a resurrection "both of the just and unjust."

The resurrection is one of God's unconditional facts; it will take place all the same though never a man, woman, or child believe in it. In regard to this alarming and comforting fact, our unbelief, neglect, cannot make the truth of God a lie. It is inevitable and irresistible. God, who cannot lie, has promised, and Jesus has sealed the promise by his resurrection.

We should familiarize ourselves with the fact. It will nerve us for the conflict of faith, bring comfort to the grave bereft of all other comfort, give a sweet and bright hope in death which destroys every other hope.

We are assured that these soul-cheering, faith-invigorating facts of the Bible are not fed upon as a sweet sacrament, cherished as our talisman against sorrow and sin. They do not enter like iron into our blood. Or else we would not be children tossed about by every wind, the prey of every temptation. This doctrine should be the joy and rejoicing of our hearts. Inspired and charmed by its hopes, we should be lifted above all weakness and defy all assaults.

We subscribe to the creed, "I believe in the resurrection of the body," which was taught by God to Moses in the burning bush, confirmed to us by prophet and apostle, symbolized and assured in the resurrection of Jesus Christ. We accept it not because we understand its method but because God has declared it in his Holy Word. To raise the dead is one of the thrilling and momentous objects of the coming of Jesus. The dead are to be raised, and Jesus Christ is coming to do that work; it is too important and glorious to be delegated to the most honored and lofty among angels or men. The Lord in person coming from heaven, with a shout of triumph and a call of authority to the heavens and to the earth.

The archangel's trump and the dead raised *first* —that is, before our Lord attends to any other business. The living are neither noticed nor crowned till the dead are awakened to share in their joys and honors. Locked in the embraces of love and reunion, we will be caught up to meet the Lord in the air, and so shall we ever be with the Lord! Amen, so let it be!

CHAPTER X

THE JUDGMENT AND THE RESURRECTION

A going-down star is not annihilated, but shall appear again. O happy and blessed death, that golden bridge laid over by Christ my Lord betwixt time's clay banks and heaven's shores!

Your sun is well turned and low; be nigh your lodging against night. We go, one by one, out of this great market till the town be empty and the two lodgings, heaven and hell, be filled. O thrice blessed are they who hold Christ with their tears and prayers!

—SAMUEL RUTHERFORD.

IT will be a resurrection. The same body which is put in the grave will come out. This is necessary to a resurrection. It is not an evolution, not a new creation, but a resurrection—a standing out and up into life again, the same body in form, substance, identity. The body is a being, a department of man's marvelous nature. It is separable from the other part of man's being, and will be separated by death. The body, its identity and being, is clear, unmistakable, well-defined, visible to eye, sensible to touch, much more tangible, visible, real to us than the soul. When death separates the spirit from the body and God says it shall return to dust, it will be so; and when God says, the body shall come out of the grave, out of its dust, the same thing we put in the grave.

The Word of God teaches that the same body which lived and died and lay in the grave will be raised—a literal resurrection, not a new creation, but a raising of the body from its grave and dust, an awakening from its long and undisturbed sleep.

The power of Christ over death was declared in the resurrection of Lazarus and his own triumph over the grave. These were prophecies, pledges, and patterns of our coming from the dead; and in each instance the same body which went into the grave came out. It shall be so with us.

The resurrection of the identical body that was laid in the grave is the doctrine of the Bible. This literal resurrection is the foundation stone of New Testament revelation. Nothing indicates our defection and driftings more than the views of the resurrection which are finding favor in high and low places among preachers, teachers, and people. With many, fiction and philosophy are substituted for the truth as it is in Jesus. We are inhaling our religious opinions from the tainted atmosphere of rationalism instead of the Bible. We are leaving Isaiah and David for Emerson or George Eliot. Robert Elsmere and John Ward preach to us instead of Paul and

Peter. We have surrendered faith to philosophy, reduced revelation to reason, and deem ourselves wiser, if not better, than our fathers. We hesitate not to say that every departure in a less or remote degree from the orthodox doctrine that the resurrection is a literal raising of the body is a departure from the Bible and a lessening of the tenacity and strength of our personal faith.

"I believe in the resurrection of the body," is Christendom's universal creed. The orthodox explanation of this item of the creed is thus summed up by Bishop Pearson: "We can therefore not otherwise expound this article than by asserting that the bodies which have lived and died shall live again after death, and that the same flesh which is corrupted shall be restored. Whatsoever alterations shall be made shall not be of their nature but of their condition, not of their substance but of their qualities; which explication is agreeable to the language of the Scripture, to the principles of religion, to the constant profession of the Church against the Origenists of old and the Socinians of late."

The Bible statement is direct, unmistakable in its meaning that these same bodies which have been the vehicles as well as the abode of the soul, its partner as well as its servant, shall be raised. The man is as much body as soul, and the Bible doctrine holds to the resurrection of the body— *this* body—its identity well maintained, and its dust rekindled to life and beauty. This same body, which has shared so fully in the trials and sorrows of this earthly life, shall share in all the ultimate triumphs or sorrows of the life to come.

In the eighth chapter of Romans we have this most explicit statement: "But if the spirit of him that raised up Jesus from the dead dwell in you, he that raised up Christ from the dead shall also quicken your mortal bodies by his Spirit that dwelleth in you." It is the mortal body, the dead body, which is to be quickened into life.

In the fifth chapter of First Thessalonians we have a prayer which has a strong bearing on this point: "And the very God of peace sanctify you wholly; and I pray God your whole spirit and soul and body be preserved blameless unto the coming of our Lord Jesus Christ." The body is to be sanctified, set apart in all its uses and members to God, sealed as his property; and in that case to be preserved blameless unto the coming of our Lord—blameless, no cause for censure, the body kept pure, free from blame.

We have the word "preserved," which means guarding, watching, take care of, to guard, to watch, to keep, as a prisoner is kept with sleepless vigilance. Who is to guard the spirit? God. Who is to guard and keep the body? God. To keep till the coming of Christ. God is to watch over the body, keep it as he keeps the spirit. So God will guard the body's sleeping dust till Jesus comes, and then bring it with him. Soul, spirit, body, kept by God's power till Jesus comes! The common and simple meaning of Scripture is that the same body will be raised from the grave. There would be no triumphant strain, triumph would not be admissible, if the body was not delivered from death! "O death, where is thy sting? O Grave, where is thy victory?" would have neither fitness nor place; but how appropriate the enrapturing notes of victory to a body laid low and humbled by the enemy death, and now released and all-victorious! The rigid Bible and orthodox view has been almost wholly surrendered by modern theology. The following will perhaps show the commonly received opinion. It is called the modern idea: "The modern doctrine repudiates this idea of a literal resurrection of the flesh. Yet it holds that the spirit has in another world some sort of organism through which it acts, and by which it has its connection with the material universe. What that organism is, and how it operates, no one pretends to know. Swedenborg held that there is in the human body a spiritual body, and that this spiritual organism rises at death, so that the soul is not yet clothed with an immortal tabernacle. This is one form of the modern doctrine of the resurrection of the body. In a sentence, then, the modern doctrine of the resurrection of the body, so far as that doctrine is in any form intelligently held, is that the spirit has in the other life a spiritual organism, and that this spiritual organism has some sort of connection, not by us understood, with the material organism which is possessed upon the earth."

CHAPTER XI

NOT ANOTHER BODY BUT THE SAME BODY

Upon the supposition that the living agent each man calls himself is a single being, it is as easy to conceive that we may hereafter animate these same or new bodies, variously modified and organized, as to conceive how we can animate such bodies as our present.
—BISHOP BUTLER.

CHURCH leaders whose standards of dictum hold to the literal resurrection have fallen in with this modern idea. The modern idea is essentially rational. It has no special regard for revelation, no great reverence for authority. The modern idea takes its cue from the Bible, but makes havoc of Bible facts and principles. It may range itself under the name of some great Bible doctrine, but it disembowels the doctrine, and leaves us nothing but an empty, delusive name. No one conversant with the trend of things can be ignorant of the fact that rationalism, under the cover of modern ideas or thought, is affecting the granite foundations of God's truth. Doctrines which the wisdom and faith of the Church have reduced to axiomatic dogmas are so changed by the transforming process of modern thought that no essential part of the original doctrine remains. The new dress has changed not only the outward appearance, but the heart of the precious old truths is entirely changed. It is marvelously strange how widespread are false views of Christ, his atonement, the resurrection of the dead, and of eternal judgment. These pernicious views are found in literature, commentary, exposition; they are clothed in such attractive garb and found in so many places that they fix themselves in thought before we are aware of it, and we have so little knowledge of the Bible that we cannot detect the counterfeit. It comes to pass that views always rejected by the great body of believers as unscriptural are referred to without scrutiny or protest.

It is one of the problems of this age to find out the process how the current of orthodoxy, purified, deepened, and made strong by the confluent piety of ages, finds itself almost lost in the shallows and sands of the ancient and worst forms of heterodoxy.

These modern ideas are not modern, though they may bear its imprint. They are almost as old as Christianity, and are as heterodox as they are old. We would not oppose them because they are new, nor reject them because they are hoary reprobates. We put no store by the modern idea. No special store do we put by the ancient idea.

We do, though, put store, all the store we can muster, by the Bible idea. We measure all that is old and all that is new by that infallible standard; and of whatever is new or whatever is old which does not agree with that, we say, Let it be accursed, and he who bids it Godspeed is partaker in the sin.

Is this modern idea the Bible idea? Is it worthy of being put to the front of gospel statements? How vague and intangible this modern idea of the resurrection! How strange that reason should reject as unworthy of credence the Bible statement of the resurrection, and yet gulp down with greediness the dreamy vagaries contained in the modern idea. The Bible idea of the resurrection of the body is the fact of a literal resurrection of the body. The Bible declares that our bodies are parts of us, that they are included in the recovering scheme of grace, that they are partners with the spirit in its earthly course of faith or disobedience, and that they are to share in the honors or shame of the eternal future.

The resurrection of the same bodies which we put in the grave is the doctrine which pervades the Bible through and through. All its truths are soaked in this great doctrine. The same body put in the grave is to come forth. Its weakness is to put on immortal energy. Its corruption is to put on incorruption. This comforting doctrine full of enrapturing, deathless hope, which has been the support of martyrs and saints, which has quenched for them the violence of the fiery stakes, which has quickened their faith, wiped away their tears, relieved the bitterness of death, and enabled them to triumph over the grave—this doctrine, which commends itself to reason as well as to faith, is to be relinquished for this modern idea, which for practical, vigorous Christian uses is as profitless as "Æsop's Fables" or the "Arabian Nights."

The Bible word to assert this doctrine is "resurrection," which means the rising again after a fall—the rising again of the thing that had fallen, not the rising of something else—and to this idea the Bible strongly and constantly holds us.

Not only is the doctrine of the resurrection of the body involved in the doctrine of the general judgment, but the fact that it is the same body. A new body could not stand in the judgment, for it is not accountable—it is the same body that was a witness and a sharer in the transactions of life that is to be in the judgment. A new body would not be amenable to the judgment bar. So it is declared that the judgment will be of the living and of the dead. "And he commanded us to preach unto the people, and to testify that it is he which was ordained of God to be the judge of quick and dead." Paul writes to Timothy: "I charge thee therefore before God, and the Lord Jesus Christ, who shall judge the quick and the dead at his appearing and his kingdom." The dead represent the ones put in the grave. Isaiah preached the resurrection of the same bodies. He was called the evangelical prophet because he saw these latter-day glories and doctrines so distinctly. He says: "Thy dead men shall live, together with my dead body shall they rise. Awake and sing, ye that dwell in dust; for thy dew is as the dew of herbs, and the earth shall cast out the dead."

The dead are to live. The body only is dead; the body is to live. With Christ's resurrection as the pattern and power they are to arise. That which dwells in the dust is to awake and sing; the body only is to be resolved to dust. The body in the dust is the body that is raised. The earth shall cast out her dead. The earth holds nothing but the body; the spirit has never been imprisoned by the earth nor soiled by its mold. The earth holds our bodies. The authority of the resurrection will break that hold, and these prisoners of hope will come forth.

supposing the fact to be allowed. Both questions, however, imply a denial of the fact, or, at least, express a strong doubt concerning it. It is thus that *"how"* in the first question is taken in many passages where it is connected with a verb; and the second question only expresses the *general* negation or doubt more particularly by implying that the objector could not conceive of any kind of body being restored to man which would not be an evil and imperfection to him. For the very reason why some of the Christians of that age denied or strongly doubted the resurrection of the body, explaining it figuratively and saying that it was past already, was, that they were influenced to this by the notion of their philosophical schools, that the body was the prison of the soul, and that the greatest deliverance men could experience was to be eternally freed from their connection with matter. Hence the early philosophizing sects in the Christian Church, the Gnostics, Marcionites, etc., denied the resurrection on the same ground as the philosophers, and thought it opposed to that perfection which they hoped to enjoy in another world. Such persons appear to have been in the Church of Corinth as early as the time of St. Paul, for that in this chapter he answers the objections not of pagans but of professing Christians appears from verse 12: "How say some among you, that there is no resurrection of the dead?" The objection, therefore, in the minds of these persons to the doctrine of the resurrection did not lie against the doctrine of the raising up of the substance of the same body; so that, provided this notion could be dispensed with, they were prepared to admit that a new material body might spring from its germ, as a plant from seed. They stumbled at the doctrine in every form, because it involved the circumstance of the reunion of the spirit with matter, which they thought an evil. When, therefore, the objector asks, "How are the dead raised up?" he is to be understood not as inquiring as to the process, but as to the possibility. The doubt may, indeed, be taken as an implied negation of the possibility of the resurrection with reference to God; and then the apostle, by referring to the springing up of the grain of corn when dissolved and putrified, may be understood to show that the event was not inconceivable by referring to God's omnipotence, as shown in his daily providence, which, *a priori,* would appear as marvelous and incredible. But it is much more probable that the impossibility implied in this question refers not to the power of God, which every Christian in the Church of Corinth must be supposed to have been taught to conceive of as almighty, and therefore adequate to the production of this effect; but as relating to the contrariety which was assumed to exist between the doctrine of the reunion of the soul with the body, and those hopes of a higher condition in a future life, which both reason and revelation taught them to form. The second question, "With what body do they come?" like the former, is a question not of inquiry but of denial, or at least of strong doubt, importing that no idea could be entertained by the objector of any material body being made the residence of a disenthralled spirit which could comport with those notions of deliverance from the bondage of corruption by death which the philosophy of the age had taught and which Christianity itself did not discountenance. The questions, though different, come, therefore, nearly to the same import; and this explains why the apostle chiefly dwells upon the answer to the latter only, by which, in fact, he replies to both. The grain cast into the earth even dies and is corrupted, and that which is sown is not "the body which shall be," in form and quality, but "naked grain"; yet into the plant, in its perfect form, is the same matter transformed. So the flesh of beasts, birds, fishes, and man is the same matter, though exhibiting different qualities. So, also, bodies celestial are of the same matter as "bodies terrestrial"; and the more splendid luminaries of the heavens are, in substance, the same as those of inferior glory. It is thus that the apostle reaches his conclusion, and shows that the doctrine of our reunion with the body implies in it no imperfection—nothing contrary to the hopes of liberation "from the burden of this flesh"

—because of the high and glorified qualities which God is able to give to matter; of which the superior purity, splendor, and energy of some material things in this world, in comparison with others, is a visible demonstration. For after he has given these instances, he adds: "So is the resurrection of the dead; it is sown in corruption, it is raised in incorruption; it is sown in dishonor, it is raised in glory; it is sown in weakness, it is raised in power; it is sown a natural [an animal] body, it is raised a spiritual body," so called, "as being accommodated to a spirit, and far excelling all that is required for the transaction of earthly and terrene affairs"; and so intent is the apostle on dissipating all those gross representations of the resurrection of the body which the objectors had assumed as the ground of their opposition, and which they had probably in their disputations placed under the strongest views, that he guards the true Christian doctrine on this point in the most explicit manner, "Now, this I say, brethren, that flesh and blood cannot inherit the kingdom of God, neither doth corruption inherit incorruption"; and, therefore, let no man henceforward affirm or assume it in his argument that we teach any such doctrine. This also he strengthens by showing that, as to the saints who are alive at the second coming of Christ, they also shall be in like manner "changed," and that "this corruptible," as to them also, "shall put on incorruption."

Thus, in the argument, the apostle confines himself wholly to the possibility of the resurrection of the body in a refined and glorified state; but omits all reference to the mode in which the thing will be effected as being out of the line of the objector's questions and in itself above human thought and wholly miraculous. It is, however, clear that when he speaks of *the body* as the subject of this wondrous "change" he speaks of it popularly as the same body in substance, whatever changes in its qualities or figure may be impressed upon it. Great general changes it will experience, as from corruption to incorruption, from mortality to immortality; great changes of a *particular* kind will also take place, as its being freed from deformities and defects, and the accidental varieties produced by climate, ailments, labor, and hereditary diseases. It is also laid down by our Lord that "in the resurrection they shall neither marry nor be given in marriage, but be like to the angels of God"; and this also implies a certain change of structure; and we may gather from the declaration of the apostle that, though "the stomach" is now adapted "to meats and meats to the stomach, God will destroy both it and them"; that the animal appetite for food will be removed, and the organ now adapted to that appetite have no place in the renewed frame. But great as these changes are, the human form will be retained in its perfection, after the model of our Lord's "glorious body," and the substance of the matter of which it is composed will not thereby be affected. That the same body which was laid in the grave shall arise out of it, is the manifest doctrine of the Scriptures.

CHAPTER XIII

BELIEF IN THE RESURRECTION AS THE CORNER STONE OF THE CHRISTIAN DISPENSATION

The resurrection of the saints is called the manifestation of the sons of God, the glorious liberty of the children of God, the adoption, the redemption of our bodies. It is the grand jubilee of the Church, and even of the creation. Till then the former as well as the latter shall be held under a degree of bondage, as being yet subject to the effects of sin. But then Christ's promise shall be fulfilled, "I will raise them up at the last day," and the deliverance of the saints will be the signal of that of the creation.
—REV. ANDREW FULLER.

THE notion of an incorruptible germ, or that of an original and unchangeable *stamen*, out of which a new and glorious body, at the resurrection, is to spring, appears to have been borrowed from the speculations of some of the Jewish rabbins, who speak of some such supposed part in the human frame under the name Luz, to which they ascribe marvelous properties and from which the body was to arise. No allusion is, however, made to any such opinion by the early fathers in their defenses of the doctrine of the resurrection from the dead. On the contrary, they argue in such a way as to prove the possibility of the *reunion* of the *scattered parts* of the body, which sufficiently shows that the germ theory had not been resorted to, by Christian divines at least, in order to harmonize the doctrine of the resurrection with philosophy. So Justin Martyr, in a fragment of his concerning the resurrection, expressly answers the objection that it is impossible for the flesh, after a corruption and perfect dissolution of all its parts, to be united together again, and contends "that if the body be not raised complete, with all its integral parts, it would argue a want of power in God"; and although some of the Jews adopted the notion of the germinating or springing up of the body from some one indestructible part, yet the most orthodox of their rabbis contended for the resurrection of the same body. So Maimonides says: "Men, in the same manner as they before lived, with the same body, shall be restored to life by God, and sent into this life with the same identity"; and "that nothing can properly be called a resurrection of the dead but the return of the very same soul into the very same body from which it was separated."

This theory, under its various forms, and whether adopted by Jews or Christians, was designed, doubtless, to render the doctrine of a resurrection from the dead less difficult to conceive, and more acceptable to philosophic minds; but, like most other attempts of the same kind to bring down the supernatural doctrines of revelation to the level of our conceptions, it escapes none of the original difficulties and involves itself in others far more perplexing.

For if by this hypothesis it was designed to remove the difficulty of conceiving how the scattered parts of one body could be preserved from becoming integral parts of other bodies, it supposes that the constant care of Providence is exerted to maintain the incorruptibility of those individual germs, or stamina, so as to prevent their assimilation with each other. Now, if they have this by original quality, then the same quality may just as easily be supposed to appertain to every particle which composes a human body; so that, though it be used for food, it shall not be capable of assimilation, in any circumstances, with another human body. But if these germs, or stamina, have not this quality by their original nature, they can be prevented from assimilating with each other only by that operation of God which is present to all his works, and which must always be directed to secure the execution of his own ultimate designs. If this view be adopted, then, if the resort must at last be to the superintendence of a Being of infinite power and wisdom, there is no greater difficulty in supposing that his care to secure this object shall extend to a million than to a thousand particles of matter. This is, in fact, the true and rational answer to the objection that the same piece of matter may happen to be a part of two or more bodies, as in the instances of men feeding upon animals which have fed upon men, and of men feeding upon one another. The question here is one which simply respects the frustrating of a final purpose of the Almighty by an operation of nature. To suppose that he cannot prevent this is to deny his power; to suppose him inattentive to it is to suppose him indifferent to his own designs; and to assume that he employs care to prevent it is to assume nothing greater, nothing in fact so great as many instances of control which are always occurring; as, for instance, the regulation of the proportion of the sexes in human births, which cannot be attributed to chance, but must either be referred to superintendence or to some original law.

Thus these theories afford no relief to the only real difficulty involved in the doctrine, but leave the whole case still to be resolved into the almighty power of God. But they involve themselves in the fatal objection that they are plainly in opposition to the doctrine of the Scriptures. For:

1. There is no resurrection of *the body* on this hypothesis, because the germ, or stamina, can in no good sense be called *"the body."* If a finger, or even a limb, is not the body, much less can these minuter parts be entitled to this appellation.

2. There is, on these theories, no resurrection at all. For if the preserved part be a germ, and the analogy of germination be adopted, then we have no longer a *resurrection* from *death*, but a *vegetation* from a suspended principle of secret *life*. If the stamina of Leibnitz be contended for, then *the body*, into which the soul enters at the resurrection, with the exception of these minute stamina, is provided for it by the addition and aggregation of new matter, and we have a *creation*, not a *resurrection*.

3. If bodies in either of these modes are to be framed for the soul by the addition of a large mass of new matter, the resurrection is made substantially the same with the pagan notion of the metempsychosis; and if St. Paul at Athens preached not "Jesus and the resurrection," but Jesus and a transmigration into a new body, it will be difficult to account for his hearers scoffing at a doctrine which had received the sanction of several of their own philosophic authorities.

Another objection to the resurrection of the body has been drawn from the changes of its substance during life. The answer to this is that, allowing a frequent and total change of the substance of the body (which, however, is but a hypothesis) to take place, it affects not the doctrine of Scripture, which is that the body which is laid in the grave shall be raised up. But, then, we are told that if our bodies have in fact undergone successive changes during life, the bodies in which we have sinned or performed rewardable actions may not be, in many instances, the same bodies as those which will be actually rewarded or punished. We answer that rewards and punishments have their relation to the body not so much as it is the *subject,* but the *instrument* of reward and punishment. It is the soul only which perceives pain or pleasure, which suffers or enjoys, and is, therefore, the only rewardable *subject*. Were we, therefore, to admit such corporeal mutations as are assumed in this objection, they affect not the case of our accountability. The personal identity or sameness of a rational being, as Mr. Locke has observed, consists in self-consciousness: "By this every one is to himself what he calls *self,* without considering whether that self be continued in the same or divers substances. It was by the same *self,* which reflects on an action done many years ago, that the action was performed." If there were indeed any weight in this objection, it would affect the proceedings of human criminal courts in all cases of offenses committed at some distance of time; but it contradicts the common sense because it contradicts the common consciousness and experience of mankind.

CHAPTER XII

A LITERAL RESURRECTION: THE BIBLE TEACHING

We converse every day with wonders and miracles no less admirable than many of those points of faith which a naturalist will not believe. .For the footprints of Omnipotence and Wisdom are in everything we see and hear: only here is the blindness of mankind, that he looks not diligently into things of ordinary occurrence, but passeth them over as of course.—LORD HALE.

THE resurrection of the body—of the same body which we put in the grave—is the corner stone of the whole Christian system. Against this doctrine the rudest assaults of unbelief have been aimed. Philosophy has held the doctrine up to scorn and contempt, as being unreasonable and impossible. The first departure from the Christian faith was the denial of the resurrection. No one doctrine of Christ's system tests the genuineness and solidity of faith as a belief in this cardinal fact. Satan generally makes the first break in faith at this point. A giving way at this point destroys the foundations. Richard Watson, whose "Theological Institutes" have been the training school of Methodist preachers for nearly a hundred years, deals with the resurrection of the body after a masterly way, with the strength of a philosopher, the simplicity and directness of a child's faith, unswerving loyalty to God's truth. He says:

In this intermediate but felicitous and glorious state the disembodied spirits of the righteous will remain in joy and felicity with Christ until the general judgment, when another display of the gracious effects of our redemption by Christ will appear in the glorious resurrection of their bodies to an immortal life, thus distinguishing them from the wicked, whose resurrection will be to "shame and everlasting contempt," or to what may be emphatically termed an immortal death.

On this subject, no point of discussion of any importance arises among those who admit the truth of Scripture, except as to the way in which the doctrine of the resurrection of the body is to be understood; whether a resurrection of the substance of the body be meant, or of some minute and indestructible part of it. The latter theory has been adopted for the sake of avoiding certain supposed difficulties. It cannot, however, fail to strike every impartial reader of the New Testament that the doctrine of the resurrection is there taught without any nice distinctions. It is always exhibited as a miraculous work, and represents the same body which is laid in the grave as the subject of this change from death to life by the power of Christ. Thus, our Lord was raised in the same body in which he died, and his resurrection is constantly held forth as the model of ours; and the apostle Paul expressly says, "Who shall change our vile body, that it may be fashioned like unto his glorious body." The only passage of Scripture which appears to favor the notion of the rising of the immortal body from some indestructible germ is 1 Corinthians xv. 35: "But some men will say, How are the dead raised up, and with what body do they come? Thou fool, that which thou sowest is not quickened except it die; and that which thou sowest, thou sowest not that body that shall be, but bare grain, it may chance of wheat, or of some other grain." If, however, it had been the intention of the apostle, holding this view of the case, to meet objections to the doctrine of the resurrection, grounded upon the difficulties of conceiving how the same body, in the popular sense, could be raised up in substance, we might have expected him to correct this misapprehension, by declaring that this was not the Christian doctrine, but that some small parts of the body only, bearing as little proportion to the whole as the germ of a seed to the plant, would be preserved, and be unfolded into the perfected body at the resurrection. Instead of this, he goes on immediately to remind the objector of the differences which exist between material bodies as they now exist: between the plant and the bare or naked grain; between one plant and another; between the flesh of men, of beasts, of fishes, and of birds; between celestial and terrestrial bodies; and between the lesser and greater celestial luminaries themselves. Still farther he proceeds to state the difference, not between the germ of the body to be raised and the body given at the resurrection, but between the body itself, understood popularly, which dies, and the body which shall be raised. "It is sown in corruption, it is raised in incorruption," which would not be true of the supposed *incorruptible* and imperishable germ of this hypothesis; and can be affirmed only of the body itself, considered in substance, and in its present state corruptible. Further, the question put by the objector, "How are the dead raised up?" does not refer to the *modus agendi* of the resurrection, or the process or manner in which the thing is to be effected, as the advocates of the germ hypothesis appear to assume. This is manifest from the answer of the apostle, who goes on immediately to state, not in what *manner* the resurrection is to be effected, but what shall be the state or condition of the resurrection body, which is no answer at all to the question, if it be taken in that sense.

The first of the two questions in the passage referred to relates to the *possibility* of the resurrection, "How are the dead raised up?" the second to the *kind of body* which they are to take, successive changes during life, the bodies in which we have sinned or performed rewardable actions may not be, in many instances, the same bodies as those which will be actually rewarded or punished. We answer that rewards and punishments have their relation to the body not so much as it is the *subject,* but the *instrument* of reward and punishment. It is the soul only which perceives pain or pleasure, which suffers or enjoys, and is, therefore, the only rewardable *subject.* Were we, therefore, to admit such corporeal mutations as are assumed in this objection, they affect not the case of our accountability. The personal identity or sameness of a rational being, as Mr. Locke has observed, consists in self-consciousness: "By this every one is to himself what he calls *self,* without considering whether that self be continued in the same or divers substances. It was by the same *self,* which reflects on an action done many years ago, that the action was performed." If there were indeed any weight in this objection, it would affect the proceedings of human criminal courts in all cases of offenses committed at some distance of time; but it contradicts the common sense because it contradicts the common consciousness and experience of mankind.

2. There is, on these theories, no resurrection at all. For if the preserved part be a germ, and the analogy of germination be adopted, then we have no longer a *resurrection* from *death,* but a *vegetation* from a suspended principle of secret *life.* If the stamina of Leibnitz be contended for, then *the body,* into which the soul enters at the resurrection, with the exception of these minute stamina, is provided for it by the addition and aggregation of new matter, and we have a *creation,* not a *resurrection.*

3. If bodies in either of these modes are to be framed for the soul by the addition of a large mass of new matter, the resurrection is made substantially the same with the pagan notion of the metempsychosis; and if St. Paul at Athens preached not "Jesus and the resurrection," but Jesus and a transmigration into a new body, it will be difficult to account for his hearers scoffing at a doctrine which had received the sanction of several of their own philosophic authorities.

Another objection to the resurrection of the body has been drawn from the changes of its substance during life. The answer to this is that, allowing a frequent and total change of the substance of the body (which, however, is but a hypothesis) to take place, it affects not the doctrine of Scripture, which is that the body which is laid in the grave shall be raised up. But, then, we are told that if our bodies have in fact undergone fact, the true and rational answer to the objection that the same piece of matter may happen to be a part of two or more bodies, as in the instances of men feeding upon animals which have fed upon men, and of men feeding upon one another. The question here is one which simply respects the frustrating of a final purpose of the Almighty by an operation of nature. To suppose that he cannot prevent this is to deny his power; to suppose him inattentive to it is to suppose him indifferent to his own designs; and to assume that he employs care to prevent it is to assume nothing greater, nothing in fact so great as many instances of control which are always occurring; as, for instance, the regulation of the proportion of the sexes in human births, which cannot be attributed to chance, but must either be referred to superintendence or to some original law.

Thus these theories afford no relief to the only real difficulty involved in the doctrine, but leave the whole case still to be resolved into the almighty power of God. But they involve themselves in the fatal objection that they are plainly in opposition to the doctrine of the Scriptures. For:

1. There is no resurrection of *the body* on this hypothesis, because the germ, or stamina, can in no good sense be called *"the body."* If a finger, or even a limb, is not the body, much less can these minuter parts be entitled to this appellation.

like most other attempts of the same kind to bring down the supernatural doctrines of revelation to the level of our conceptions, it escapes none of the original difficulties and involves itself in others far more perplexing.

For if by this hypothesis it was designed to remove the difficulty of conceiving how the scattered parts of one body could be preserved from becoming integral parts of other bodies, it supposes that the constant care of Providence is exerted to maintain the incorruptibility of those individual germs, or stamina, so as to prevent their assimilation with each other. Now, if they have this by original quality, then the same quality may just as easily be supposed to appertain to every particle which composes a human body; so that, though it be used for food, it shall not be capable of assimilation, in any circumstances, with another human body. But if these germs, or stamina, have not this quality by their original nature, they can be prevented from assimilating with each other only by that operation of God which is present to all his works, and which must always be directed to secure the execution of his own ultimate designs. If this view be adopted, then, if the resort must at last be to the superintendence of a Being of infinite power and wisdom, there is no greater difficulty in supposing that his care to secure this object shall extend to a million than to a thousand particles of matter. This is, in the dead. On the contrary, they argue in such a way as to prove the possibility of the *reunion* of the *scattered parts* of the body, which sufficiently shows that the germ theory had not been resorted to, by Christian divines at least, in order to harmonize the doctrine of the resurrection with philosophy. So Justin Martyr, in a fragment of his concerning the resurrection, expressly answers the objection that it is impossible for the flesh, after a corruption and perfect dissolution of all its parts, to be united together again, and contends "that if the body be not raised complete, with all its integral parts, it would argue a want of power in God"; and although some of the Jews adopted the notion of the germinating or springing up of the body from some one indestructible part, yet the most orthodox of their rabbis contended for the resurrection of the same body. So Maimonides says: "Men, in the same manner as they before lived, with the same body, shall be restored to life by God, and sent into this life with the same identity"; and "that nothing can properly be called a resurrection of the dead but the return of the very same soul into the very same body from which it was separated."

This theory, under its various forms, and whether adopted by Jews or Christians, was designed, doubtless, to render the doctrine of a resurrection from the dead less difficult to conceive, and more acceptable to philosophic minds; but,

CHAPTER XIII

BELIEF IN THE RESURRECTION AS THE CORNER STONE OF THE CHRISTIAN DISPENSATION

The resurrection of the saints is called the manifestation of the sons of God, the glorious liberty of the children of God, the adoption, the redemption of our bodies. It is the grand jubilee of the Church, and even of the creation. Till then the former as well as the latter shall be held under a degree of bondage, as being yet subject to the effects of sin. But then Christ's promise shall be fulfilled, "I will raise them up at the last day," and the deliverance of the saints will be the signal of that of the creation.
—Rev. Andrew Fuller.

The notion of an incorruptible germ, or that of an original and unchangeable *stamen*, out of which a new and glorious body, at the resurrection, is to spring, appears to have been borrowed from the speculations of some of the Jewish rabbins, who speak of some such supposed part in the human frame under the name Luz, to which they ascribe marvelous properties and from which the body was to arise. No allusion is, however, made to any such opinion by the early fathers in their defenses of the doctrine of the resurrection from are, the human form will be retained in its perfection, after the model of our Lord's "glorious body," and the substance of the matter of which it is composed will not thereby be affected. That the same body which was laid in the grave shall arise out of it, is the manifest doctrine of the Scriptures.

corruptible," as to them also, "shall put on incorruption."

Thus, in the argument, the apostle confines himself wholly to the possibility of the resurrection of the body in a refined and glorified state; but omits all reference to the mode in which the thing will be effected as being out of the line of the objector's questions and in itself above human thought and wholly miraculous. It is, however, clear that when he speaks of *the body* as the subject of this wondrous "change" he speaks of it popularly as the same body in substance, whatever changes in its qualities or figure may be impressed upon it. Great general changes it will experience, as from corruption to incorruption, from mortality to immortality; great changes of a *particular* kind will also take place, as its being freed from deformities and defects, and the accidental varieties produced by climate, ailments, labor, and hereditary diseases. It is also laid down by our Lord that "in the resurrection they shall neither marry nor be given in marriage, but be like to the angels of God"; and this also implies a certain change of structure; and we may gather from the declaration of the apostle that, though "the stomach" is now adapted "to meats and meats to the stomach, God will destroy both it and them"; that the animal appetite for food will be removed, and the organ now adapted to that appetite have no place in the renewed frame. But great as these changes

—because of the high and glorified qualities which God is able to give to matter; of which the superior purity, splendor, and energy of some material things in this world, in comparison with others, is a visible demonstration. For after he has given these instances, he adds: "So is the resurrection of the dead; it is sown in corruption, it is raised in incorruption; it is sown in dishonor, it is raised in glory; it is sown in weakness, it is raised in power; it is sown a natural [an animal] body, it is raised a spiritual body," so called, "as being accommodated to a spirit, and far excelling all that is required for the transaction of earthly and terrene affairs"; and so intent is the apostle on dissipating all those gross representations of the resurrection of the body which the objectors had assumed as the ground of their opposition, and which they had probably in their disputations placed under the strongest views, that he guards the true Christian doctrine on this point in the most explicit manner, "Now, this I say, brethren, that flesh and blood cannot inherit the kingdom of God, neither doth corruption inherit incorruption"; and, therefore, let no man henceforward affirm or assume it in his argument that we teach any such doctrine. This also he strengthens by showing that, as to the saints who are alive at the second coming of Christ, they also shall be in like manner "changed," and that "this in a future life, which both reason and revelation taught them to form. The second question, "With what body do they come?" like the former, is a question not of inquiry but of denial, or at least of strong doubt, importing that no idea could be entertained by the objector of any material body being made the residence of a disenthralled spirit which could comport with those notions of deliverance from the bondage of corruption by death which the philosophy of the age had taught and which Christianity itself did not discountenance. The questions, though different, come, therefore, nearly to the same import; and this explains why the apostle chiefly dwells upon the answer to the latter only, by which, in fact, he replies to both. The grain cast into the earth even dies and is corrupted, and that which is sown is not "the body which shall be," in form and quality, but "naked grain"; yet into the plant, in its perfect form, is the same matter transformed. So the flesh of beasts, birds, fishes, and man is the same matter, though exhibiting different qualities. So, also, bodies celestial are of the same matter as "bodies terrestrial"; and the more splendid luminaries of the heavens are, in substance, the same as those of inferior glory. It is thus that the apostle reaches his conclusion, and shows that the doctrine of our reunion with the body implies in it no imperfection—nothing contrary to the hopes of liberation "from the burden of this flesh" of these persons to the doctrine of the resurrection did not lie against the doctrine of the raising up of the substance of the same body; so that, provided this notion could be dispensed with, they were prepared to admit that a new material body might spring from its germ, as a plant from seed. They stumbled at the doctrine in every form, because it involved the circumstance of the reunion of the spirit with matter, which they thought an evil. When, therefore, the objector asks, "How are the dead raised up?" he is to be understood not as inquiring as to the process, but as to the possibility. The doubt may, indeed, be taken as an implied negation of the possibility of the resurrection with reference to God; and then the apostle, by referring to the springing up of the grain of corn when dissolved and putrified, may be understood to show that the event was not inconceivable by referring to God's omnipotence, as shown in his daily providence, which, *a priori,* would appear as marvelous and incredible. But it is much more probable that the impossibility implied in this question refers not to the power of God, which every Christian in the Church of Corinth must be supposed to have been taught to conceive of as almighty, and therefore adequate to the production of this effect; but as relating to the contrariety which was assumed to exist between the doctrine of the reunion of the soul with the body, and those hopes of a higher condition supposing the fact to be allowed. Both questions, however, imply a denial of the fact, or, at least, express a strong doubt concerning it. It is thus that *"how"* in the first question is taken in many passages where it is connected with a verb; and the second question only expresses the *general* negation or doubt more particularly by implying that the objector could not conceive of any kind of body being restored to man which would not be an evil and imperfection to him. For the very reason why some of the Christians of that age denied or strongly doubted the resurrection of the body, explaining it figuratively and saying that it was past already, was, that they were influenced to this by the notion of their philosophical schools, that the body was the prison of the soul, and that the greatest deliverance men could experience was to be eternally freed from their connection with matter. Hence the early philosophizing sects in the Christian Church, the Gnostics, Marcionites, etc., denied the resurrection on the same ground as the philosophers, and thought it opposed to that perfection which they hoped to enjoy in another world. Such persons appear to have been in the Church of Corinth as early as the time of St. Paul, for that in this chapter he answers the objections not of pagans but of professing Christians appears from verse 12: "How say some among you, that there is no resurrection of the dead?" The objection, therefore, in the minds

CHAPTER XIV

RESURRECTION OF THE BODY COMPLETE

Who for the first time saw the little pendant coffin in which the insect lay entombed would ever predict that in a few weeks, perhaps in a few days or hours, it would become one of the most elegant and active of winged insects? And who that contemplates with the mind of a philosopher this curious transformation and knows that two years before the insect mounts into the air, even while it is living in water, it has the rudiment of wings, can deny that the body of a dead man may at some future period be again invested with vigor and activity and soar to regions for which some latent organization may have peculiarly fitted it?—DR. GREGORY.

JOHN WESLEY, who has the undisputed premiership in the great Methodist movement, holds to the doctrine of the resurrection in an inflexible and scriptural way. In a sermon from the fifteenth chapter of First Corinthians he says:

The apostle, having in the beginning of this chapter firmly settled the truth of our Saviour's resurrection, adds: "Now if Christ be preached that he rose from the dead, how say some among you that there is no resurrection of the dead?" It cannot now any longer seem impossible to you that God should raise the dead; since you have so plain an example of it in our Lord, who was dead and is alive; and the same power which raised Christ must also be able to quicken our immortal bodies.

"But some man will say, How are the dead raised up? and with what body do they come?" How can these things be? How is it possible that these bodies should be raised again and joined to their several souls, which many thousands of years ago were either buried in the earth or swallowed up in the sea or devoured by fire?—which have moldered into the finest dust, that dust scattered over the face of the earth, dispersed as far as the heavens are wide—nay, which has undergone ten thousand changes, has fattened the earth, become the food of other creatures, and these again the food of other men? How is it possible that all these little parts, which made up the body of Abraham, should be again ranged together, and, unmixed with the dust of other bodies, be all placed in the same order and posture that they were before, so as to make up the very selfsame body which his soul at his death forsook? Ezekiel was indeed, in a vision, set down in a valley full of dry bones, "and he heard a noise, and behold a shaking, and the bones came together, bone to his bone; the sinews and the flesh came upon them, and the skin covered them above, and breath came into them, and they lived, and stood upon their feet." This might be in a vision. But that all this, and much more, should in time come to pass; that our bones after they are crumbled into dust should really become living men; that all the little parts whereof our bodies were made should immediately, at a general summons, meet again, and every one challenge and possess its own place, till at last the whole be perfectly rebuilt—that this, I say, should be done is so incredible a thing that we cannot so much as have any notion of it. And we may observe that the Gentiles were most displeased with this article of the Christian faith. It was one of the last things the heathens believed, and it is to this day the chief objection to Christianity.

It may be proper to mention some of the reasons upon which this article of our faith is built.

The plain notion of a resurrection requires that the selfsame body that died should rise again. Nothing can be said to be raised again but that very body that died. If God give to our souls at the last day a new body, this cannot be called the resurrection of our body, because that word plainly implies the fresh production of what was before.

There are many places of Scripture that plainly declare it. St. Paul, in the fifty-third verse of this chapter, tells us that "This corruptible must put on incorruption, and this mortal must put on immortality." Now by this mortal and this corruptible can be meant only that body which we now carry about with us, and shall one day lay down in the dust.

The mention which the Scripture makes of the places where the dead shall rise further shows that the same body which died shall rise. Thus we read in Daniel: "Those that sleep in the dust of the earth shall awake; some to everlasting life, and some to shame and everlasting contempt." And we may likewise observe that the very phrase of *sleep* and *awake* implies that when we rise again from the dead our bodies will be as much the same as they are when we awake from sleep. Thus again our Lord affirms: "The hour is coming in which all that are in the graves shall hear his voice and shall come forth; they that have done good to the resurrection of life, and they that have done evil to the resurrection of damnation." (John v. 28, 29.) Now if the same body do not rise again, what need is there of opening the graves at the end of the world? The graves can give up no bodies but those which were laid in them. If we were not to rise with the very same bodies that died, then they might rest forever. To this we need only add that of St. Paul: "The Lord shall change this vile body, that it may be fashioned like unto his glorious body." Now this vile body can be no other than that with which we are now clothed, which must be restored to life again.

That in all this there is nothing incredible or impossible, I shall show by proving these three things: (1) That it is possible for God to keep and preserve unmixed from all other bodies the particular dust into which our several bodies are dissolved, and can gather and join it again, how far soever dispersed asunder. (2) That God can form that dust so gathered together into the same body it was before. (3) That when he hath formed this body he can enliven it with the same soul that before inhabited it.

1. God can distinguish and keep unmixed from all other bodies the particular dust into which our several bodies are dissolved, and can gather it together and join it again, how far soever dispersed asunder. God is infinite both in knowledge and power. He knoweth the number of the stars, and calleth them all by their names; he can tell the number of the sands on the seashore; and is it at all incredible that he should distinctly know the several particles of dust into which the bodies of men are moldered, and plainly discern to whom they belong and the various changes they have undergone? Why should it be thought strange that he, who at the first formed us, whose eyes saw our substance yet being imperfect, from whom we were not hid when we were made in secret and curiously wrought in the lowest parts of the earth, should know every part of our bodies and every particle of dust whereof we were

composed? The artist knows every part of the watch which he frames; and if it should fall in pieces, and the various parts of it lie in the greatest disorder and confusion, yet he can soon gather them together and as easily distinguish one from another as if every one had its particular mark. He knows the use of each, and can readily give it its proper place and put them all exactly in the same figure and order they were before. And can we think that the Almighty Builder of the world, whose workmanship we are, does not know whereof we are made or is not acquainted with the several parts of which this earthly tabernacle is composed? All these lay in one vast heap at the creation till he separated them one from another and framed them into those distinct bodies whereof this beautiful world consists. And why may not the same power collect the ruins of our corrupted bodies and restore them to their former condition? All the parts into which men's bodies are dissolved, however they seem to us carelessly scattered over the face of the earth, are yet carefully laid up by God's wise disposal till the day of the restoration of all things. They are preserved in the waters and fires, in the birds and beasts, till the last trumpet shall summon them to their former habitation.

But say they: "It may sometimes happen that several men's bodies may consist of the selfsame matter. For the bodies of men are often devoured by other animals, which are eaten by other men. Nay, there are nations which feed upon human flesh; consequently they borrow a great part of their bodies from other men. And if that which was part of one man's body becomes afterwards part of another man's, how can both rise at the last day with the same bodies they had before?" To this it may easily be replied that a very small part of what is eaten turns to nourishment; the far greater part goes away according to the order of nature. So that it is not at all impossible for God, who watches over and governs all this, so to order things that what is part of one man's body, though eaten by another, shall never turn to his nourishment; or if it does, that it shall wear off again, and sometime before his death be separated from him, so that it may remain in a capacity of being restored at the last day to its former owner.

2. God can form this dust, so gathered together, into the same body it was before. And that it is possible all must own who believe that God made Adam out of the dust of the earth. Therefore the bodies of men being dust after death, it is no other than it was before; and the same power that at the first made it of dust may as easily remake it when it is turned into dust again. Nay, it is no more wonderful than the forming of a human body in the womb, which is a thing we have daily experience of, and is doubt-

less as strange an instance of divine power as the resurrection of it can possibly be. And were it not so common a thing, we should be as hardly brought to think it possible that such a beautiful fabric as the body of man is, with nerves and bones, flesh and veins, blood, and the several other parts whereof it consists, should be formed, as we know it is, as now we are, that hereafter it should be rebuilt when it has been crumbled into dust. Had we only heard of the wonderful production of the bodies of men, we should have been as ready to ask: "How are men made, and with what bodies are they born?" as now, when we hear of the resurrection, "How are the dead raised up, and with what bodies do they come?"

3. When God hath raised this body, he can enliven it with the same soul that inhabited it before. And this we cannot pretend to say is impossible to be done, for it has been done already. Our Saviour himself was dead, rose again, and appeared alive to his disciples and others, who had lived with him many years, and were then fully convinced that he was the same person they had seen die upon the cross.

Thus have I shown that the resurrection of the same body is by no means impossible to God. That which he hath promised he is able also to perform by that "mighty power by which he is able to subdue all things to himself." Though, therefore, we cannot exactly tell the manner how it shall be done, yet this ought not in the least to weaken our belief of this important article of our faith. It is enough that he to whom all things are possible hath passed his word that he will raise us again. Let those who presume to mock at the glorious hope of all good men, and are constantly raising objections against it, first try their skill upon the various appearances of nature. Let them explain everything which they see happen in this world before they talk of the difficulties of explaining the resurrection. Can they tell me how their own bodies were fashioned and curiously wrought? Can they give me a plain account, by what orderly steps this glorious, stately structure, which discovers so much workmanship and rare contrivance, was at first created? How was the first drop of blood made, and how came the heart and veins and arteries to receive it? Of what and by what means were the nerves and fibers made? What fixed the little springs in their due places, and fitted them for the several uses for which they now serve? How was the brain distinguished from the other parts of the body and filled with spirits to move and animate the whole? How came the body to be fenced with bones and sinews, to be clothed with skin and flesh, distinguished into various muscles? Let them but answer these few questions about the mechanism of our own bodies, and I will answer all the difficulties concerning the resurrection of them. But if they cannot do this without having recourse to the infinite power and wisdom of the First Cause, let them know that the same power and wisdom can reanimate it after it is turned into dust, and that there is no reason for our doubting concerning the thing because there are some circumstances belonging to it which we cannot perfectly comprehend or give a distinct account of.

CHAPTER XV

WESLEY'S ARGUMENT FOR A RESURRECTION AND NOT A CREATION

This he [Paul] calls the manifestation of the sons of God, alluding to children's being brought forth to the light when they are born. This was to have its highest fulfillment at the resurrection, when they shall be born from the grave. They themselves, therefore, join with the creation around them, groaning within themselves, waiting for the most glorious, the ultimate and perfect manifestation of the sons of God when they shall be born of the grave.—REV. JONATHAN EDWARDS.

THEN John Wesley shows the change between the qualities of the mortal and glorified bodies of God's saints. He says:

The change which shall be made in our bodies at the resurrection, according to the Scripture account, will consist chiefly in these four things: (1) That our bodies shall be raised immortal and incorruptible. (2) That they shall be raised in glory. (3) That they shall be raised in power. (4) That they shall be raised spiritual bodies.

1. The body that we shall have at the resurrection shall be immortal and incorruptible: "For

this corruptible must put on incorruption, and this mortal must put on immortality." Now these words "immortal" and "incorruptible" not only signify that we shall die no more (for in that sense the damned are immortal and incorruptible), but that we shall be perfectly free from all the bodily evils which sin brought into the world. That our bodies shall not be subject to sickness or pain or any other inconveniences we are daily exposed to. This the Scripture calls "the redemption of our bodies," the freeing them from all their maladies. Were we to receive them again, subject to all the frailties and miseries which we are forced to wrestle with, I much doubt whether a wise man, were he left to his choice, would willingly take his again—whether he would not choose to let his still lie rotting in the grave rather than to be again chained to such a cumbersome clod of earth. Such a resurrection would be, as a wise heathen calls it, "a resurrection to another sleep." It would look more like a redemption to death again than a resurrection to life.

The best thing we can say of this house of earth is, That it is a ruinous building, and will not be long before it tumbles into dust; that it is not our home (we look for another house eternal in the heavens); that we shall not always be confined here, but that in a little time we shall be delivered from the bondage of corruption, from this burden of flesh, into the glorious liberty of the sons of God. What frail things these bodies of ours are! How soon are they disordered! To what a troop of diseases, pains, and other infirmities are they constantly subject! And how does the least distemper disturb our minds and make life itself a burden! Of how many parts do our bodies consist! And if one of these be disordered, the whole man suffers. If but one of these slender threads whereof our flesh is made up be stretched beyond its due proportion, or fretted by any sharp humor, or broken, what torment does it create! Nay, when our bodies are at the best, what pains do we take to answer their necessities, to provide for their sustenance, to preserve them in health, and to keep them tenantable, in some tolerable fitness for our soul's use. And what time we can spare from our labor is taken up in rest and refreshing our jaded bodies and fitting them for work again. How are we forced, even naturally, into the confines of death; even to cease to be; at least to pass so many hours without any useful or reasonable thoughts, merely to keep them in repair! But our hope and comfort are that we shall shortly be delivered from this burden of flesh, when "God shall wipe away all tears from our eyes, and there shall be no more death, neither sorrow, nor crying, neither shall there be any more pain; for the former things are passed away." O when shall we arrive at that happy land where no complaints were ever heard, where we shall all enjoy uninterrupted health both of body and mind, and nevermore be exposed to any of those inconveniences that disturb our present pilgrimage? When we shall have once passed from death unto life, we shall be eased of all the troublesome care of our bodies, which now takes up so much of our time and thoughts. We shall be set free from all those mean and tiresome labors which we must now undergo to support our lives. Yon robes of light, with which we shall be clothed at the resurrection of the just, will not stand in need of those careful provisions which it is so troublesome to us here either to procure or to be without. But then, as our Lord tells us, those who shall be accounted worthy to obtain that world neither marry nor are given in marriage, neither can they die any more, but they are equal to the angels. Their bodies are neither subject to disease, nor want that daily sustenance which these mortal bodies cannot be without. "Meats for the belly, and the belly for meats; but God will destroy both it and them." This is that perfect happiness which all good men shall enjoy in the other world: a mind free from all trouble and guilt in a body free from all pains and diseases. Thus our mortal bodies shall be raised immortal. They shall not only be always preserved from death (for so these might be, if God pleased), but the nature of them shall be wholly changed so that they shall not retain the same seeds of mortality: they cannot die any more.

2. Our bodies shall be raised in glory. "Then shall the righteous shine as the sun in the kingdom of their Father." A resemblance of this we have in the luster of Moses's face when he had conversed with God on the mount. His face shone so bright that the children of Israel were afraid to come near him till he threw a veil over it. And that extraordinary majesty of Stephen's face seemed to be an earnest of his glory. "All that sat in the council, looking steadfastly on him, saw his face as it had been the face of an angel." How then, if it shone so gloriously even on earth, will it shine in the other world, when his and the bodies of all the saints are made like unto Christ's glorious body! How glorious the body of Christ is, we may guess from his transfiguration. St. Peter, when he saw this, when our Lord's face shone as the sun and his raiment became shining and white as snow, was so transported with joy and admiration that he knew not what he said. When our Saviour discovered but a little of that glory which he now possesses, and which in due time he will impart to his followers, yet that little of it made the place seem a paradise; and the disciples thought that they could wish for nothing better than always to live in such pure light and enjoy so beautiful a sight. "It is good for us to be here: let us make three tabernacles." Here let

us fix our abode forever. And if they thought it so happy only to be present with such heavenly bodies and to behold them with their eyes, how much happier must it be to dwell in such glorious mansions and to be themselves clothed with so much brightness!

This excellency of our heavenly bodies will probably arise in a great measure from the happiness of our souls. The unspeakable joy that we then shall feel will break through our bodies and shine forth in our countenances. As the joy of the soul even in this life has some influence upon the countenance, by rendering it more open and cheerful, so Solomon tells us: "A man's wisdom makes his face to shine." Virtue, as it refines a man's heart, so it makes his very looks more cheerful and lively.

3. Our bodies shall be raised in power. This expresses the sprightliness of our heavenly bodies, the nimbleness of their motion, by which they shall be obedient and able instruments of the soul. In this state our bodies are no better than clogs and fetters, which confine and restrain the freedom of the soul. The corruptible body presses down the soul, and the earthly tabernacle weighs down the mind. Our dull, sluggish, inactive bodies are often unable, or backward, to obey the commands of the soul. But in the other life "they that wait upon the Lord shall renew their strength; they shall mount up with wings as eagles, they

shall run and not be weary, they shall walk and not faint." Or, as another expresses it: "They shall run to and fro like sparks among the stubble." The speed of their motion shall be like that of devouring fire in stubble, and the height of it above the towering of an eagle; for they shall meet the Lord in the air, when he comes to judgment, and mount up with him into the highest heaven. This earthly body is slow and heavy in all its motions, listless, and soon tired with action. But our heavenly bodies shall be as fire, as active and as nimble as our thoughts are.

4. Our bodies shall be raised spiritual bodies. Our spirits are now forced to serve our bodies and to attend their leisure, and do greatly depend upon them for most of their actions. But our bodies shall then wholly serve our spirits and minister to them and depend upon them. So that as by a natural body we understand one fitted for this lower, sensible world, for this earthly estate, so a spiritual body is one that is suited to a spiritual state, to an invisible world, to the life of angels. And, indeed, this is the principal difference between a mortal and a glorified body. This flesh is the most dangerous enemy we have: we therefore deny and renounce it in our baptism. It constantly tempts us to evil. Every sense is a snare to us. All its lusts and appetites are inordinate. It is ungovernable, and often rebels against reason. The law in our members wars

against the law of our mind. When the spirit is willing, the flesh is weak; so that the best of men are forced to keep it under and use it hardly lest it should betray them into folly and misery. And how does it hinder us in all our devotions! How soon does it jade our minds when employed on holy things! How easily by its enchanting pleasures does it divert them from those noble exercises! But when we have obtanied the resurrection unto life, our bodies will be spiritualized, purified, and refined from their earthly grossness. Then they will be fit instruments for the soul in all its divine and heavenly employment; we shall not be weary of singing praises to God through infinite ages.

Thus after what little we have been able to conceive of it, it sufficiently appears that a glorified body is infinitely more excellent and desirable than this vile body.

CHAPTER XVI

THE CHRISTIAN'S BODY RAISED IMMORTAL AND INCORRUPTIBLE

The resurrection of the dead must be admitted to be a great mystery which nothing but the occurrence of the fact can unfold. The apostle puts this question into the mouth of an infidel: "How are the dead raised up? and with what body do they come?" which he answers in a very unceremonious manner: "Thou fool, that which thou sowest is not quickened, except it die: and that which thou sowest, thou sowest not that body that shall be, but bare grain, it may chance of wheat, or of some other grain: but God giveth it a body as it hath pleased him, and to every seed his own body." The glorious prospect opened by this doctrine is not less animating because it surpasses our comprehension. On the contrary, its profundity only serves to increase our astonishment and enhance our gratitude. The apostle, in his apology before Felix, resolves the whole into an immediate exertion of divine power. Why should it be thought a thing incredible that God should raise the dead? If indeed the gospel professed to teach the theory of the fact, it would be a just objection that this was beyond the grasp of our faculties. If, on the contrary, it merely reveals facts and those facts have immediate practical bearings on the hearts and lives of those who receive them, all objections on account of their mysteriousness are futile, because they proceed on the supposition that God intends to develop the whole mystery,

whereas He discovers only so much as may be adapted to rectify the conscience and purify the heart.
—Robert Hall.

John Wesley concludes by practical inferences:

1. From what has been said, we may learn the best way of preparing ourselves to live in those heavenly bodies, which is by cleansing ourselves more and more from all earthly affections, and weaning ourselves from this body and all the pleasures that are peculiar to it. We should begin in this life to loosen the knot between our souls and this mortal flesh; to refine our affections, and raise them from things below to things above; to take off our thoughts and disengage them from present and sensible things, and accustom ourselves to think of and converse with things future and invisible; that so our souls, when they leave this earthly body, may be prepared for a spiritual one, as having beforehand tasted spiritual delights and being in some degree acquainted with the things which we then shall meet with. A soul wholly taken up with this earthly body is not fit for the glorious mansions above. A sensual mind is so wedded to bodily pleasures that it cannot enjoy itself without them, and it is not able to relish any other, though infinitely to be preferred before them. Nay, such as follow the inclinations of their fleshly appetites are so far unfit for

heavenly joys that they would esteem it the greatest unhappiness to be clothed with a spiritual body. It would be like clothing a beggar in the robes of a king. Such glorious bodies would be uneasy to them; they would not know what to do in them; they would be glad to retire and put on their rags again. But when we are washed from the guilt of our sins, and cleansed from all filthiness of flesh and spirit, by faith in the Lord Jesus Christ, then we shall long to be dissolved and to be with our exalted Saviour. We shall be always ready to take wing for the other world, where we shall at last have a body suited to our spiritual appetites.

2. From hence we may see how to account for the different degrees of glory in the heavenly world. For although all the children of God shall have glorious bodies, yet the glory of them all shall not be equal. "As one star differeth from another star in glory, so also is the resurrection of the dead." They shall all shine as stars, but those who, by a constant diligence in well-doing, have attained to a higher measure of purity than others shall shine more brightly than others. They shall appear as more glorious stars. It is certain that the most heavenly bodies will be given to the most heavenly souls; so that this is no little encouragement to us to make the greatest progress we possibly can in the knowledge and love of God, since the more we are weaned from the things

of the earth now the more glorious will our bodies be at the resurrection.

3. Let this consideration engage us patiently to bear whatever troubles we may be exercised with in the present life. The time of our eternal redemption draweth nigh. Let us hold out a little longer, and all tears shall be wiped from our eyes and we shall never sigh nor sorrow any more. And how soon shall we forget all we endured in this earthly tabernacle, when once we are clothed with that house which is from above? We are now but on our journey toward home, and so must expect to struggle with many difficulties; but it will not be long ere we come to our journey's end, and that will make amends for all. We shall then be in a quiet and safe harbor, out of the reach of all storms and dangers. We shall then be at home in our Father's house, no longer exposed to the inconveniences which, so long as we abide abroad in these tents, we are subject to. And let us not forfeit all this happiness for want of a little more patience. Only let us hold out to the end, and we shall receive an abundant recompense for all the trouble and uneasiness of our passage, which shall be endless rest and peace.

Let this especially fortify us against the fear of death; it is now disarmed, and can do us no hurt. It divides us indeed from this body awhile, but it is only that we may receive it again more glorious. As God therefore said once to Jacob,

"Fear not to go down into Egypt, for I will go down with thee, and will surely bring thee up again," so I may say to all who are born of God, Fear not to go down into the grave: lay down your heads in the dust; for God will certainly bring you up again, and that in a much more glorious manner. Only "be ye steadfast and unmovable, always abounding in the work of the Lord," and then let death prevail over and pull down this house of clay; since God hath undertaken to rear it up again, infinitely more beautiful, strong and useful.

We see how this apostle and founder of Methodism held to the Bible statement of this vital and fundamental fact. Had John Wesley held the fact of the resurrection of the body by a feeble or a lax tenure, then he would neither have been God's apostle nor the founder of Methodism. Wesleyan Methodism had not been if John Wesley had gingerly held this essential and indispensable fact dissolved and disemboweled by philosophical admixture and rationalistic dubiety. All this marvelous work would not have been, or gone glimmering—"A schoolboy's tale, the wonder of an hour;" "Like a tale told by an idiot; full of sound and fury signifying nothing."

We have made these extracts from men of the highest order of intellect and culture of varied creeds of faith, yet essentially one. We see that they accepted the fact of the resurrection of the body as their gospel creed, maintained it despite all philosophical objections, and heartily approved and advocated it.

We would reëmphasize the fact that there are no new arguments nor stronger ones against the resurrection of the body than those which the fathers had to confront, and they met them with resolute and strong faith. Why is this doctrine held so feebly and with so many qualifications by the Church of this day? There is no solution of this question to be found outside of the decay of that simple, spiritual, strong faith which dominated these men who made their times a great spiritual era.

These men spent no time nor devices in devising methods to make it easy for God to seem to do what he had promised to do and yet not do it. By the modern popular process of tinkering and toning we get God out of the matter, and reduce the Christian system to a godless philosophy. A resurrection without God is the point to which modern progressive theology is moving. It is high time we had quit this toning down divine truth to answer the purposes of our unfaith and bad philosophy. This is a poor business for preachers or people to be at—this playing the rôle of philosophers, this dwarfing and destroying revelation to satisfy the limitations and blindness of reason. Let reason use all its sanctified powers in ascertaining what God says, in learning in silence, reverence, and meekness God's words—learn to obey revelation, but never to sit in judgment on its truth, its fitness, nor its facts.

CHAPTER XVII

SOME BODIES WILL SHINE MORE BRIGHTLY THAN OTHERS

We may think, perchance, that we are free to speculate to prove historical credibilities, to boast the liberty of a suspended assent to what seems all too objective and material for the falsely spiritualizing tendencies of the age in which we live. We may think so now; but when the end draws near, when sorrow breaks us, when age weakens, when darkness begins to close around us, where will all such license of thought be and what will it avail us?
—BISHOP ELLICOTT.

AMID the signs and transactions of the death and resurrection of Christ we have this statement: "And the graves were opened; and many bodies of the saints which slept arose, and came out of the graves after his resurrection, and went into the holy city, and appeared unto many."

The graves were opened, the bodies that slept arose and came out of their graves. Nothing could be more explicit; nothing clearer than that this was a literal resurrection, a literal return to life of the bodies put in the grave. This is the first fruit of Christ's resurrection, the pledge and symbol of ours.

Christ's resurrection was the great pattern of ours. He said to his disciples: "Behold, my hands and my feet, that it is I myself, handle me and see." He showed them his hands and side— a literal resurrection of his pierced, marred, and bleeding body. This is the earnest authority and hope of our resurrection. We are to be raised from the dead, not from a germ, for this is the fact paganized. It is not a rehabilitation, not a new creation, but a raising up again of the same thing which had fallen—raised and transfigured, refined, glorified, in conditions, relations, qualities. So also is the resurrection of the dead.

Among the first indications of heresy is that about the resurrection; our going off begins here. In Paul's masterly argument in Corinthians to refute these resurrection heretics, he sets forth the literal resurrection: the body sown in weakness, raised in power; the same body raised that is sown. The mortal—that is, the dead body— puts on immortality. The corruptible body puts on incorruption.

The dead are to stand before God in judgment. We are to be judged for the deeds done in this body. This body is a partner in all our doing, and it must bear its share in the awards of that judgment day. Christ says soul and body can be cast by God into hell. The identity, the unity, and sameness follow through the history of eternity. These vile bodies are to be changed—not other bodies made, but these we bear and will put in the grave are to feel the regenerating and transforming force of the resurrection.

Daniel says: "And many of them that sleep in the dust of the earth shall awake, and some to everlasting life, and some to shame and everlasting contempt."

The sleepers are to come forth. It is the body that sleeps; the soul never sleeps. It is that which is sleeping in the dust of the earth which is to awake. The sleepers in the dust of the earth are to awake. The body only is sleeping in the dust of the earth. What could be more specific, direct, than this statement?

Our Lord says: "Marvel not at this: for the hour is coming, in the which all that are in the graves shall hear his voice, and shall come forth; they that have done good, unto the resurrection of life, and they that have done evil, unto the resurrection of damnation."

Here the resurrection is coming out of the grave. What have we put in the grave? These mortal bodies—and that which we put in the grave is to hear his voice and come out of the grave.

Paul puts the doctrine in a wholesome form and very full of comfort: "But I would not have you to be ignorant, brethren, concerning them which are asleep, that ye sorrow not, even as others which have no hope. For if we believe that Jesus died and rose again, even so them also which sleep in Jesus will God bring with him."

No refining in this to meet the vicious philosophy of the day. No surrender to the higher rationalistic and Sadducean criticism. It is a brave and tender statement of a precious and divine truth. Who are sleeping in Christ? We know who! We folded their hands with tears and kissed the lips and laid them to sleep and wrote on their tombs the words of hope and resurrection. We did not see their spirits and could not follow them in their heavenward flight, but we did bear their bodies, broken-hearted, and lay them to sleep and their forms are forever mirrored on our hearts, and Christ shall bring them back to us out of their graves and out of their sleep to our embrace and to our hearts.

We sang, as we laid them to sleep, "Asleep in Jesus." We put it on the marble that marked their bed of sleep:

> "Asleep in Jesus! Blessed sleep!
> From which none ever wakes to weep."

It is out of the grave they are to come! It is out of the dust they are to come! It is out of the sea they are to come! The body is in the grave, the body is in the dust, the body is in the sea. The body, imperishable as the spirit, shall by the voice of the Son of God come out of the grave, come out of the dust, come out of the sea.

Glorious fact, mysterious fact; but God, God's Son, God's Word makes and solves its mystery. Faith holds to God, faith holds to God's Son, faith holds to God's Word. Faith, almighty faith, sees God, sees the Son of God, sees his word, laughs at mysteries and impossibilities, and cries: "It shall be done!"

CHAPTER XVIII

CHRIST'S RESURRECTION THE PLEDGE AND SYMBOL OF OURS

Paul felt in the depths of his soul that the life of the Christian, as it subsists in faith now, can only subsist in hope of the future. Without this assumed view of the future, the whole Christian life appears in his eyes as endeavors without an object, the pursuit of a phantom, the sport of a delusion. For the life of other men is directed to the higher or lower aims which are to be attained in intellectual pursuits, or in the gratification of the senses and which can be actually attained on earth. But the life of Christians, with all its conflicts, efforts, and renunciations, refers to an object that has no truth, if it be not realized in the eternal life of the future.
—JOHANN A. W. NEANDER.

IT is obvious that this present body, not in substance but in qualities and capacity, will not be suited to the changed and higher conditions and employments of the heavenly life. It may not be so obvious, but must be equally true that the revelation on this point, if made to us in detail, could not be understood, and so we have the facts stated in an explicit but general way, that these bodies are to be changed. The great outlines only are given. It is said with force that these bodies in their present qualities will be entirely unsuited to the changed relations; that flesh and blood cannot inherit that happy state nor meet its high demands.

Speculations and theories, never satisfactory, are generally profitless in regard to these divine mysteries. The Bible is the only safe guide. We are not to seek after mysteries in God's Word, or marvels, but to search out and know the truth as revealed by God in its teaching without error, fancy, human opinion, or philosophy. God's truth is all we need to know. It is what we ought to want and earnestly and faithfully to seek.

God reveals to us two distinct facts about his purposes with our bodies: The first is the raising of our bodies from the grave. The body is his in its original creation: he made it fearfully and wonderfully. This body is sacred to God; sacred to God by creation. God created these bodies. Out of common dust they were made, but the dust was sanctified and made holy for God's high purposes. The body is sacred to God, for it is his temple, as sacred and holier than any temple ever built to God: "Know ye not that your body is a temple of the Holy Ghost which is in you?" The body dedicated as a temple is devoted to God. The body holy to God as a temple is holy. Our bodies are God's work, God's workmanship, God's temple, God's property. He owns these bodies; they are to glorify him and he will glorify them. The body is sacred to God because he clothed his Son in it. Jesus wore this body on earth, wears it now in heaven. The body shares in the work of the redemption by Jesus; its regeneration will come through its resurrection and glorious change. God sanctified and ennobled it by appearing *in the body* to patriarch and prophet. He gave it divine honor and clothed it with immortality when he clothed his Son in a body of flesh. He gave the body triumph when he raised it from the dead in the person of his Son. This body he has declared he will raise from the deadly ravages of the grave. The second great purpose God has in decree for the body is that it shall be so changed as to qualify it for and adapt it to all the highest enjoyments, employments, pursuits, and advantages of the heavenly life.

This change so marvelous may be likened to the regeneration of our souls. The substance is not changed, the identity and sameness not destroyed, but a wonderful transformation has taken place in the conditions, relations, appetencies of the soul. The man is the same, and yet a new man; old things are passed away, and behold, all things are become new. This change which comes over the body may be likened to that which comes over the earth when the deadness and coldness of winter give way to the life, beauty, and warmth of spring; it seems a different world, so changed from glory to glory, and yet it is the same, but we see what God can work. The same God who works such regenerating wonders in the soul, such natural wonders in the transforming spring—this same God shall awake these dead bodies from the sleep and wreck of the grave and regenerate them into glories far more abiding and sublime than these which mark the changing spring. Amen! So let it be!

We have no adequate idea of the change; imagination has scarcely a foundation on which to build, fancy must not be indulged. Our ordinary language and conceptions are tame and cannot rise to the height of this mysterious and thrilling fact. The Bible gives us the model and some outlines. The model is the glorious body of Christ. The model we have never seen. Its picture was shown to us on the Mount of Transfiguration, but we are blinded and stupefied by its glory. The outlines of this great change which is to come upon our bodies is given us in the fifteenth chapter of First Corinthians. We there learn that the change will make it a powerful body, not in the enlargement of size, but in the elements of force, endurance, energy. It will have neither inherent nor acquired tendency to decay; its vigor will be unimpaired, its energy never relaxed. Corruption will put on incorruption. Death will be swallowed up in life. Dimness, dishonor, shame will be changed to glory. The change will be from a natural, earthly body to a spiritual, heavenly one. The body, so the Bible teaches us, will come out of the grave changed into immortal strength, never to know weariness, weakness, tears, decay, death, ready for the different and higher uses of the heavenly life.

The change will not be by stages or progressions—no evolution in it—but in a moment, in the twinkling of an eye, when the last trump shall sound. The change will be by the immediate power of God, distinct from the resurrection in fact and act, but scarcely in time. This is our faith: the resurrection of the body by the power of God. We live in this faith; we bury our dead by the light of this hope; shall fall asleep ourselves with this blissful hope as our winding sheet.

CHAPTER XIX

THIS CHANGED BODY WILL NEVER KNOW WEAKNESS, TEARS OR DECAY

We are informed that both Moses and Elijah appeared also in glory!—a glory somewhat similar, we may suppose, though far inferior, to that with which Christ was invested. Like him, they were probably clothed in raiment of unusual whiteness and splendor; and the form of their countenances might also be changed to something brighter and more illustrious. Now this would be a just representation of the glorified state of saints in heaven. Particular attestation was given on the mount to two of its principal doctrines: a general resurrection and a day of retribution.—BISHOP PORTEUS.

THE change will not be in material substance nor shape. Christ was of the same form, shape, and substance after his resurrection as before, but refined, glorified. The marvelous change is based simply on the power of God, who, out of the same substance and material, can make so many diverse things. Many most serious, pernicious errors have had their origin in the failure to discriminate between the two—the resurrection of the body and its miraculous change. The error among some Corinthians about the doctrine of the resurrection seems to be the modern idea that this body, earthly, dull, low, and fleshly in its nature and appetencies, was thereby unfitted for the heavenly life, and would not be raised. The Bible comes in and says it will be changed and refined in substance—not new, but changed to meet changed conditions. The husband builds a house ample and well fitted to his uses when first married, family small; but when the family enlarges and conditions change, with ample means he does not build a new house, but out of the substance and material of the old he changes his home.

Paul avers God's ability to change the body by referring to nature in seed-sowing. The farmer in his wheat sows a bare grain; God is able to take that grain of wheat and so alter it that it comes out in a blade and stalk—the body that God chooses to give it. Then God takes the substance—flesh, mere flesh—and he changes some of it into the highest order of flesh, flesh of men; then he changes the same substance into a coarser fabric, flesh of beasts, another flesh of fishes, and another part he fashions flesh of birds—showing God's power to endlessly diversify the same substance. Then God's ability extends to make out of the same material heavenly bodies for heavenly uses, and earthly bodies for earthly uses. Not only does God's illimitable power extend to diversifying the same flesh into various kinds, not only does his power enable him to make out of the same substance bodies for low earthly uses and also for high heavenly uses; but the power by which he can diversify and make the same substance diverse in its glory, like the sun, moon, and stars, all the same in substance and form but different in glory by God's power. So the argument that God can change the elements and material of this body make it all glorious. So he replies to the heterodox Corinthian who in the spirit of unfaith asked: "How are the dead raised up? and with what body do they come?" Raised up, says Paul, by the power of God, and changed, says Paul, to fit the demands of the resurrection life.

We have the distinct and luminous statement in Philippians: "For our citizenship is in heaven; from whence also we wait for a Saviour, the Lord Jesus Christ: who shall fashion anew the body of our humiliation, *that it may be* conformed to the body of his glory, according to the working whereby he is able even to subject all things unto himself."

The time of the change will be at the second coming of our Lord Jesus Christ. "For the Lord himself shall descend from heaven, with the voice of the archangel and with the trump of God: and the dead in Christ shall rise first." And he (the Lord Jesus Christ) will fashion anew this body of our humiliation—the old body. The pattern of new fashioning of our bodies will be his own glorious body, nothing higher, nothing richer, nothing diviner, nothing more beautiful than the glorified body of Jesus. We have in the transfiguration of Jesus a glance at his glorious body. As Trench says: "The transfiguration has ever been contemplated in the Church as a prophecy of the glory which the saints shall have in the resurrection. As was the body of Christ on the mount, so hereafter shall their bodies be. In passages out of number we have hints of the luminous character of the future glorified bodies of the redeemed. All these scriptures pointing to the glorious conformity of their bodies then, with all which his body at this time was, who now showed in himself as the first fruits of the new creation what hereafter he would show in all them that were his." How luminous his body the night of the transfiguration! They describe it: "His face did shine as the sun, his garments became white as the light." "His garments became glistering, exceeding white; so as no fuller on earth can whiten them." "And as he was praying, the fashion of his countenance was altered, and his raiment became white and dazzling." Glory was there! Moses and Elijah appeared in glory.

The pattern after which our resurrection will be found is the glorified body of Christ. This is not only hinted at, but distinctly asserted in the Bible: "And so it is written, The first man,

Adam, was made a living soul; the last Adam was made a quickening spirit. Howbeit that was not first which is spiritual, but that which is natural; and afterwards that which is spiritual. The first man is of the earth, earthy; the second man is the Lord from heaven. As is the earthy, such are they also that are earthy; and as is the heavenly, such are they also that are heavenly. And as we have borne the image of the earthy, we shall also bear the image of the heavenly."

CHAPTER XX

AND AS WE HAVE BORNE THE IMAGE OF THE EARTHY, WE SHALL ALSO BEAR THE IMAGE OF THE HEAVENLY

How shall dust and ashes hope to ascend into the heaven of heavens if it cannot feel with all the fullness of conviction that One who was bone of our bone and flesh of our flesh has entered those realms before us and has taken up our very nature glorified and beautified to the right hand of the Everlasting Father?—BISHOP ELLICOTT.

THE Bible declares that these bodies are to be changed, not other bodies made or developed; but these vile bodies, the earthly bodies which belonged to us, the bodies of our humiliation, shame, and weakness, are to be changed and fashioned into the form of Christ's glorious body. It was Christ's same body, the body pierced and dead on the cross, the body which slept in Joseph's tomb that was made glorious. So it is to be our same body—the body which had suffered the humiliation—that is to share the glory. It is to be accomplished by his divine power, and at his second coming.

This change will follow, in point of time, immediately after the resurrection. The change will not be secured by the gracious effects of the genial clime nor advanced by the slow stages of progress. It will be instantaneous, the immediate act of God's creative and regenerating power.

This will be the hour of our final triumph; the last enemy, Death, will be destroyed, and no traces of the ravages of death nor the ruin of sin will be left. Then we will have proof of the correctness of the apostle's figuring and its results: "For I reckon that the sufferings of this present time are not worthy to be compared with the glory which shall be revealed in us."

Then will be realized the transmuting power of God—how the dull and dreary things of this life can be changed to jeweled brightness; how its light afflictions, which pressed so wearily and heavily upon us, have been working for us a far more exceeding and eternal weight of glory. Then we shall not see through this earthy glass darkly, but face to face, with full and unveiled vision; then, in the fullness of knowledge as well as light, we shall know even as we are known. Then we will realize how here, even with the highest spiritual vision, eye did not see, nor ear hear, neither did it enter into the heart of man to conceive of things which God hath prepared for them that love him.

These are the two glorious facts awaiting these bodies—these bodies broken and imprisoned even in this life and humbled into death and dust. They are to be raised from the dead, the long sleep of death is to be broken by the power of God when the archangel's trump shall sound; but it also teaches that the body thus raised shall undergo a change to fit it for its glorious resurrection life. Paul declares to us that this change shall consist of several particulars, which shall distinguish it from and contrast it with the present body, described by him thus: "It is sown in corruption; it is raised in incorruption." Changed from corruption to incorruption. Our bodies now are wasted, wasted by sickness, wasted by age, wasted by care, wasted by toil. All, everything, mark it as corruptible—its beauty fades, its strength decays, its life grows feeble and feebler. Our heavenly bodies will not be subject to decay nor to the weakness of age; they will not be the heirs of sickness or death; by them

> "Sickness and sorrow, pain and death
> Will be felt and feared no more."

Sorrow and the labors of this earthly life break and mar the force of this body and it wastes away. Our resurrection body will not be affected by any of these.

"It is sown in dishonor; it is raised in glory." Dishonor, ignominy, disgrace, the grave, the dirt, the rottenness. We bury our dead out of our sight, dishonored, lost to sight, surrendered to darkness, loneliness, silence, to rottenness, worms, and to earth, to ashes, to dust.

These bodies are dim and dishonored things, bodies of humiliation, shame, and suffering; they arrest the full flow of joy and check the rapture of the immortal spirit. The transformation which they will undergo will make them glorious, shining with a splendor which outvies the sun. Doubtless they will be luminous and attractive, shapely with symmetry and perfect in form, lustrous with an immortal life, radiant with its deathless charms.

Do we overstate the change: *Raised in glory?* Glory, magnificence, excellence, preëminence, dignity, grace, splendor, brightness—these all, each, are in it. Christ said of them: "They shall shine forth as the sun in the kingdom of their Father." "They that be wise shall shine as the brightness of the firmament; and they that turn many to righteousness as the stars forever and ever."

CHAPTER XXI

OUR BODIES CHANGED INSTANTANEOUSLY AT SECOND COMING OF CHRIST

I rejoice in the glory to be revealed, for it is no uncertain glory we look for. Our hope is not hung upon such an untwisted thread as I imagine so, or it is likely, but the cable of the strong tow of our fastened anchor is the oath and promise of Him who is eternal verity. Our salvation is fastened with God's own hand, with Christ's own strength, to the strong strap of God's unchangeable nature.

Let us be ballasted with grace that we be not blown over and that we stagger not. I never believed till now that there was so much to be found in Christ on this side of death and heaven. How sweet, how sweet is our investment!—SAMUEL RUTHERFORD.

"It is sown in weakness; it is raised in power." Our bodies in their present form are feeble. Their history is sown in weakness, frailty is the essential quality, their greatest vigor is dashed in a moment's disease, its manliest strength goes down to childish feebleness in a day and sinks helpless and nerveless into the grave—born to weakness, as well as to sorrow, as the sparks fly upward. The resurrection change will be into power. Energy will be one of its predominant features then, as weakness is now—energy, deathless energy; energy unimpaired by labor, by clime, by sickness, or death; energy without restraint or diminution, energy tireless in its pursuits. Exhaustless in its flow of life and spirits, it will need no rest to repair, no sleep to refresh, no recreation to recover waste; it will feel no faintness nor fatigue by the strongest pressure, severest tension, and most engaging employments. They will serve God day and night, as the outflow of a vigor which is sustained without pain or weariness through all the midday hours of that nightless land.

Weariness, weakness, waste are here. The heavenly bodies will be strength unabated, vigor unworn, life unweakened; no age to its youth, no sickness to its health, no fatigue to its toil, no night to its day. Energy unabated, power unlimited, strength unimpaired, vigor unweakened—these will characterize our heavenly bodies.

"It is sown a natural body; it is raised a spiritual body." Natural, our present bodies are akin to the brutes and in common with them—subject to appetite and passion, not actuated by the higher part of our being. The spiritual body will be lifted above appetite, passion, fitted for the uses and as the vehicle of the immortal part of man which is akin to God, and all its being, uses, and employment must be after God's high and heavenly designs. These bodies of ours in their present form are natural bodies, fitted for our present uses, but low and fleshly in their tastes and tendencies. They are but dragged unwillingly into the regions of the spiritual and heavenly; they are truly of the earth earthy—"vile bodies" they are called in the Epistle to the Philippians. The change will fit them for heavenly and spiritual uses; they will be the fitting agents for the changed, high, happy sphere into which the resurrection life has introduced them. The fittest organs they will be for heavenly activities and heavenly engagements. These earthborn and earth-habituated bodies translated to heaven without change would be unfit for the engagements of that world, bewildered by its brightness, appalled by its sleepless labors. Smitten and overpowered by its ecstatic visions, they could not bear the strain of that life; they could not engage in its worship nor meet the duties of one hour of heavenly demands. Its change will fit it for the exchange of weakness for strength, sickness for health, life for death, and mortality for immortality, earth for heaven.

The apostle begins this fifteenth chapter of First Corinthians to refute errors about the doctrine of the resurrection, but carries it on by putting the doctrine in its true and sublime attitude, and closes with a lofty and triumphant strain: "If there is a natural body, there is also a spiritual body. So also it is written, The first man, Adam, became a living soul. The last Adam became a life-giving spirit. Howbeit that is not first which is spiritual, but that which is natural; then that which is spiritual. The first man is of the earth, earthy: the second man is of heaven. As is the earthy, such are they also that are earthy: and as is the heavenly, such are they also that are heavenly. And as we have borne the image of the earthy, we shall also bear the image of the heavenly. Now this I say, brethren, that flesh and blood cannot inherit the kingdom of God; neither doth corruption inherit incorruption. Behold, I tell you a mystery: We shall not all sleep, but we shall all be changed, in a moment, in the twinkling of an eye, at the last trump: for the trumpet shall sound, and the dead shall be raised incorruptible, and we shall be changed. For this corruptible must put on incorruption, and this mortal must put on immortality. But when this corruptible shall have put on incorruption, and this mortal shall have put on immortality, then shall come to pass the saying that is written, Death is swallowed up in victory. O death, where is thy sting? O grave, where is thy victory? The sting of death is sin; and the power of sin is the law: but thanks be to God, which giveth us the victory through our Lord Jesus Christ. Wherefore, my beloved brethren, be ye steadfast, unmovable, always abounding in the work of the Lord, forasmuch as ye know that your labor is not vain in the Lord."

Here the apostle includes in this great change those who are living when Christ shall come. Though they do not die, they will be changed—that is, those who are Christ's. In a moment, quicker than thought, the work will be wrought; the change not in substance but in quality. At that time, the bodies of the dead in every particle rescued from the grave and changed to incorruption, the triumph will be complete. Then, and not till then, our rapturous and victorious song will be sung, and the prophecy fulfilled.

CHAPTER XXII

WEARINESS, WASTE, WEAKNESS HERE—DEATHLESS ENERGY THERE

Figuratively speaking, when Christ slipped down from the cross, He descended first "into the lower parts of the earth" and came into the kingdom of death. With one stroke of His mighty sword He cut away the turrets and foundations of death's temple. With another sweep of that terrible scimetar He broke death's scepter, smashed his crown, captured his keys, then plunging through the ashes of damnation and lunging on the gates of hell, tore them from their sockets, cutting the bars of iron in pieces and ascending the throne of his imperial majesty the devil, He hurled him into the burning marl and sulphurous flame, then placing His right foot upon the neck of the devil and His left upon the jaws of death, He lifted his hand to heaven and shouted through the gloom of eternal night "I am He that liveth and was dead; and behold I am alive forevermore and have the keys of death and hell." And in a moment more with Satan chained to one chariot wheel and death to the other, He drove up the steeps of Hades leading captivity captive while heaven's hosts peering over the battlemented walls of jasper shouted in raptured choruses, "He hath prevailed, He hath prevailed; He shall not fail, He shall not fail." Emerging at a point called Joseph's Tomb and remaining forty days with his friends He after this ascended into heaven "from whence we look for the Saviour: the Lord Jesus Christ: who shall change our vile body that it may be fashioned

like unto His glorious body, according to the working whereby he is able even to subdue all things unto himself."
—Rev. Homer W. Hodge.

The future of man will be divinely glorious and divinely illustrious. He is to share the place of Jesus, where Jesus and his followers are to be. This is the specific teaching of Jesus. "I go to prepare a *place* for you," said Jesus; "and if I go and prepare a *place* for you, I come again, and will receive you unto myself; *that where I am, there ye may be also."* In his sacerdotal prayer Jesus said: "Father, that which thou hast given me, I will that, where I am, they also may be with me; that they may behold my glory, which thou hast given me." The statement in the Apocalypse is very exalted, very strong, and very clear: "He that overcometh, I will give to him to sit down with me in my throne, as I also overcame, and sat down with my Father in his throne."

Jesus must have the place of greatest dignity, of highest honor in the universe. God has awarded this to him without question or limitation—a name above every name, a place above every place. Jesus calls it paradise, a place of ineffable beauty, God-adorned and exuberant in its divine embellishments—untold beauty to fascinate the eye and ravish and intoxicate the heart. The divine word is that Jesus will shepherd all the blessed flock of that thrice-blessed land. With them Jesus will be, and for them Jesus will be.

The honor, dignity, power, and glory bestowed on him will be theirs. They are joint heirs with him of all God's most generous inheritance. Rich indeed, surpassing rich, shall be the saints in that large, exhaustless, immortal store.

"I am fully persuaded of this as of a most necessary and infallible truth: that as it is appointed unto all men once to die, so it is determined that all men shall rise from death, that the souls separated from our bodies are in the hands of God and live, that the bodies dissolved into dust or scattered into ashes shall be recollected in themselves and reunited to their souls, that the same flesh which lived before shall be revived, that the same numerical bodies which did fall shall rise, that this resuscitation shall be universal, no man excepted, no flesh left in the grave, that all the just shall be raised to a resurrection of life, and all the unjust to a resurrection of damnation; that this shall be performed at the last day when the trump shall sound, and this I believe the resurrection of the body."

With what acclamations with saints, rising from the dead, applaud the Redeemer! How will the heaven of heavens resound his praises forever! "Thanks be to God" will be the burden of their song; and angels will join in the chorus and declare their consent with a loud AMEN! HALLELUJAH!